# COOPERATION
# &
# COERCION

**HOW BUSYBODIES BECAME BUSYBULLIES
AND WHAT THAT MEANS FOR
ECONOMICS AND POLITICS**

ANTONY DAVIES AND
JAMES R. HARRIGAN

I S I
BOOKS

WILMINGTON, DE

Library of Congress Control Number: 2019957405

ISBN: 978-1-61017-156-4

Published in the United States by

ISI Books
Intercollegiate Studies Institute
3901 Centerville Road
Wilmington, DE 19807-1938
www.isibooks.org

Manufactured in the United States of America

For Maggie, Kristina, and Chloe: the three women in my life who have always had more faith in me than I in myself.
—A. D.

For my family, Johanne, Fiona, Sophia, Patrick, and Molly. And for my inadvertent life partner, Antony Davies.
—J. H.

# CONTENTS

Introduction     Cooperation and Coercion     9

Part 1     How We Got Here

1     The Knowledge Problem     19
2     Rights and Wrongs     37
3     The Magic Wand     47

Part 2     Cooperation and Coercion in Everyday Life

4     The Minimum Wage     63
5     Gun Control     83
6     Wars on Nouns     103
7     Taxes     119
8     Debt     135
9     Busybullies     151
10     Cooperation     163

Notes     179
Acknowledgments     195
Index     197

# COOPERATION AND COERCION

There are only two ways that humans work together: they cooperate with one another, or they coerce one another.

That's it. Every nonsolitary endeavor humans have undertaken since the dawn of the species has employed cooperation, coercion, or some combination of these two organizing principles.

Cooperation is voluntary. In cooperation, people freely come together to form groups. They devise rules for how those in the group should behave. People are free to leave the group; people are free to ask to join the group; people within the group are free to accept new members or not, and to kick out members. Cooperative groups enforce rules by mutually agreed association. If a person does not abide by the group's rules, people within the group may choose not to associate with the person. The important point is that cooperation requires the consent of all parties.

A business, for example, is a cooperative group. A person joins a business as an employee only by the mutual consent of the person and the employer. The person cannot force the employer to hire him, and the employer cannot force the person to accept a job at the business. Both employee and employer agree to abide by certain rules, but either can free himself from those rules at any time—the employee by quitting, the employer by firing the employee.

Similarly, churches, civic organizations, social clubs, and even Friday night poker games are cooperative groups.

Coercion is involuntary. It occurs when a person (or a group of people) restricts the autonomy of another person, typically through violence or the threat of violence. Because coercive groups ultimately enforce rules by physical might, they do not require the consent of their members.

Coercion is not always bad. Yes, murdering, stealing, and polluting all involve coercion—but so does *preventing* people from murdering, stealing, and polluting. When humans want to apply coercion in a good way, government is the tool they use.

A government is a coercive organization. A person born into a society is automatically subject to the rules that the society's government imposes. Sometimes the person can leave, but only by physically moving his household and, even then, only with the permission of both the government whose territory he is leaving and the government whose territory he proposes to enter.

Clearly, dictatorships are coercive. But so, too, are democracies.

What separates a dictatorship and a democracy is the number of people required to decide whether and how to coerce. In a democracy, 50 percent of the voters plus one can impose their wills on the remainder of the population. If only 50 percent of the population votes, as is typical in the United States, then "50 percent of the voters" is actually 25 percent of the population imposing its will on everyone else.[1] We all abide by rules, including plenty that we don't agree with, in the name of getting along.

## The Pursuit of Happiness

Three of the greatest philosophical minds humanity has ever produced, Aristotle, Immanuel Kant, and John Stuart Mill, disagreed significantly on many things, but each believed that people's ultimate goal was to become happy and that everything everyone does is ultimately in service to this. Though they had radically different ideas about *how* to attain happiness, they agreed that the *goal* is happiness. As Aristotle says, man is a social animal, so human beings have to live with one another in peace to be fully human, to be happy.

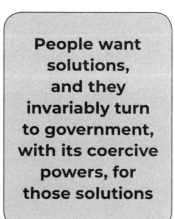

**People want solutions, and they invariably turn to government, with its coercive powers, for those solutions**

The important question is how best to do that: through cooperation or coercion?

The benefit of cooperation is that people may choose whether to participate. This makes cooperative behavior self-correcting, because people will tend to want to cooperate in ventures that increase their happiness and to avoid ventures that do not. Businesses with quality products, low prices, and friendly service will tend to attract customers. Churches whose congregations are unwelcoming or judgmental will tend to lose members. Neighborhoods that are well kept and friendly will tend to attract residents.

The benefit of coercion is that people may not decline to participate. We do not want people deciding for themselves whether to murder, steal, or defraud. Being peaceful, respecting people's property, and behaving honestly are behaviors we want to be universal. Coercion can yield uniform behavior. When abused, it can, and almost always does, yield all kinds of other behaviors, too. Uniform behavior is desirable only if the people subject to the coercion agree on what things will yield happiness and if the coercers know best how to attain those things. Here is where things get tricky.

Take the example of murder again. Almost everyone agrees that less murder yields more happiness, and an effective way to attain less murder is for would-be murderers to know that they will be caught and severely punished. Hence, preventing murder via incarceration is a good application for coercion. But what about banning firearms? Is that an effective way to achieve lower murder rates? Is such a ban a good application for coercion? On these issues there is significant disagreement.

Apart from a handful of obvious examples, almost all of which involve one person inflicting harm on another, it's pretty hard to reach agreement on what objectives yield happiness. More city parking might make drivers happy, but bikers or pedestrians will not be thrilled with increased automobile traffic. Steel tariffs are great for domestic steelworkers but not for domestic autoworkers, whose employers must pay more for steel, or for domestic car buyers, who must pay more for cars.

Things get even trickier when we remember that human beings are at once individuals worthy of respect and members of a shared society that can and does make significant demands on them. Here the difference between government and society is laid bare. Government is a coercive tool society employs to achieve certain ends. Society, on the other hand, is the aggregation of people themselves, and is generally cooperative. When people consider government and society to be the same, they end up understanding neither.

Perhaps no one got to the heart of the difference, especially in the United States, better than Thomas Paine in 1776:

> Society in every state is a blessing, but government even in its best state is but a necessary evil; in its worst state an

intolerable one; for when we suffer, or are exposed to the same miseries by a government, which we might expect in a country without government, our calamity is heightened by reflecting that we furnish the means by which we suffer. Government, like dress, is the badge of lost innocence; the palaces of kings are built on the ruins of the bowers of paradise. For were the impulses of conscience clear, uniform, and irresistibly obeyed, man would need no other lawgiver; but that not being the case, he finds it necessary to surrender up a part of his property to furnish means for the protection of the rest; and this he is induced to do by the same prudence which in every other case advises him out of two evils to choose the least. Wherefore, security being the true design and end of government, it unanswerably follows that whatever form thereof appears most likely to ensure it to us, with the least expense and greatest benefit, is preferable to all others.[2]

Society, according to Paine, is always a blessing. Government is difficult because it carries enough power to make us miserable, which it sometimes does.

Nonetheless, government is necessary. On this point nearly every great thinker agrees, but no one put it more clearly than Thomas Jefferson in the Declaration of Independence. There, like Paine, he asserted that government exists to effect the safety and happiness of the people, which it does by securing their rights. This is the quintessential duty of government. And "whenever any Form of Government becomes destructive of these ends," Jefferson held, "it is the Right of the People to alter or to abolish it, and to institute new Government, laying its foundation on such principles and organizing its powers in such form, as to them shall seem most likely to effect their Safety and Happiness." For Jefferson, having no government was not an option.

He might have stopped short of Paine's assertion that government was a "necessary evil," but he stopped just short of it.

## How Much Can Government Accomplish?

Aristotle started with human nature and arrived at the inevitability of government in short order. On the North American continent in the eighteenth century, Paine and Jefferson came quickly to see government as necessary but dangerous. And this point of view held sway for much of American history. But as we will see, things have changed quite a bit in recent decades. Coercion is almost the default position now.

Just look at political campaigns. Voters demand to know how candidates will use the power of government to solve every problem under the sun. And candidates oblige by publishing five-point plans for addressing a startling array of issues. College tuitions are too high? The government needs to step in. Healthcare needs to improve? The government needs to step in. America needs more affordable housing? Or healthier diets? Or to increase manufacturing? Or to end the opioid crisis? Or to reduce gun violence? The government needs to step in.

People want solutions, and they want them now. And they invariably turn to government, with its coercive powers, for those solutions.

But these new expectations obscure government's purpose as well as its limitations. In the end, government exists to protect the rights of individuals. It does not exist to protect society, least of all from itself. This is because society is not something that *can be* protected. Society emerges from the interactions of its members over time. "Protecting society" has no real meaning, precisely because society is always a work in progress. It is constantly refining itself. To "protect society" would be to freeze it, or some aspect of it, in place. This would destroy society by contradicting its very nature. So when we use coercive methods in an attempt to "protect society" rather than the individuals who comprise it, we end up with offenses like the Salem witch trials, the Trail of Tears, black chattel slavery, and Japanese internment. This sort of inhumanity requires political authority. The power to imprison, enslave, and kill are powers only governments can claim. And individuals can imprison, enslave, and kill others with impunity only when they do so under the aegis of government.

The essence of government is force. From waging war to issuing parking tickets, every government action manifests either violence or the threat of violence for those who do not comply. Voluntary association is the tool society uses when its members are free to behave as they will. Government is the tool society uses to force its members to behave in certain ways. Cloaking the tool in the civility of democracy does not change its essence. Government is a necessary and often useful tool—but it is also an extremely dangerous one.

In the pages that follow, we examine the dual forces of cooperation and coercion as they play out against a backdrop of human nature, on the one hand, and human activity on the other. We take as axiomatic, following Aristotle, that human beings are by nature social creatures, that they are designed to live together. What the human race has managed to accomplish, and it has accomplished great things, has come about as a result of man's social nature—that is, as a result of cooperation.

We also take as axiomatic that human beings, all of them, are deeply imperfect creatures whose behavior must, more than occasionally, be restrained. As beautiful and productive as cooperation is, coercion is a necessary ingredient when human beings decide how best to live together.

The operative question, always, is when should we coerce our fellow citizens and when should we step back and allow them to cooperate. There is no hard and fast rule that will answer this question in every instance, but as we will see, patterns of human behavior do, in fact, emerge. Those patterns clearly indicate that when government limits its force to preventing people from harming one another, people have the maximum ability to cooperate. And although coercion is sometimes necessary, ultimately cooperation is the key to human progress. The more we encourage cooperation, the better off we all will be.

# PART 1

# HOW WE GOT HERE

# 1

# THE KNOWLEDGE PROBLEM

People want more in exchange for less. This is a reality of human nature that holds whether people operate in a capitalist, socialist, communist, or any other environment. And it holds whether people work in the for-profit world, in the nonprofit world, for government, or not at all. Because it's impossible for anyone to receive anything without someone, somewhere, paying a price, humans developed economic and political systems for figuring out who gets what, who pays, and how they pay. Some systems have worked well and some have worked poorly. Constructing a workable system requires knowing many things.

Everywhere one looks, one sees evidence of accumulated human knowledge. Human beings live in relative comfort in desert climates and in the inhospitable cold. Medical technology yields longer lives than people even two generations ago could have thought possible. We can manipulate food at the genetic level so more of us can eat well at lower cost. Satellites ring the earth to allow better communications and entertainment, and even to give us directions when we get lost. The overwhelming majority of adults and many children in the Western world have smartphones, each of which contains more computing power than NASA had at its disposal when it put people on the moon. On those smartphones we can watch live video being broadcast half a world away, listen to music, and even occasionally talk to other people.

But for all that we know collectively, each one of us, even the smartest of us, actually doesn't know much. This is the knowledge problem, and it took one of the brightest lights the human race ever produced to recognize the problem.

Socrates lived almost 2,500 years ago, yet his wisdom remains so relevant that it is nearly impossible to graduate college without reading about him. Much of what we know about him comes through the works of his student Plato, but one can find contemporaneous accounts of him in Xenophon and the playwright Aristophanes, and secondary accounts in countless works written since. Socrates is almost universally regarded as one of the smartest people who ever lived.

Yet Socrates described himself very differently.

Shortly before his death, he told the story of his friend Chaerephon, who went to the Oracle at Delphi and asked whether anyone was wiser than Socrates. The Oracle answered no, no one was wiser. This was lost on Socrates himself, who claimed, "I know that I have no wisdom, small or great." But how could the Oracle at Delphi, who spoke on behalf of the god himself, possibly be wrong?

Socrates decided to question the people of Athens, find someone wiser than himself, and return to the Oracle with that person in tow as evidence of his own ignorance. But a curious thing happened when he tried to find a person wiser than himself: he couldn't find one. He questioned many people with reputations for wisdom, including politicians, philosophers, poets, and artisans. He found that although many Athenians considered these people wise, and those people thought themselves wiser still, they weren't. Socrates concluded that if he were truly wise, it was precisely because he knew his own limitations. He never claimed to know any more than he actually knew.

Compare Socrates to just about every member of the political class today. Political orientation scarcely matters. Nearly everyone, Republican, Democrat, or Independent, who aspires to political office, from small-town mayor to President of the United States, begins his political journey with the belief that he knows best how other people should live. Not surprisingly, it is the goal of every politician to inflict his knowledge on the rest of us. And why not? If he really knows how people should live, why wouldn't he try to impose his ideas on the rest of us?

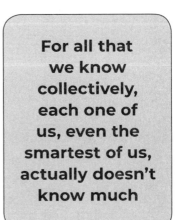

For all that we know collectively, each one of us, even the smartest of us, actually doesn't know much

Was Socrates right, or should we follow the lead of virtually every politician who ever lived?

To think about that question, we should turn our attention to... pencils?

## I, Pencil

In a short 1958 essay, economist Leonard Read made a fantastic claim. No one, he said, could make something as simple as a pencil all by himself. This sounds ridiculous on its face. Pencils are so inexpensive that people do not even care when you take one from them and wander away with it. Pencils are ubiquitous, so how could Read claim that no one person, living or dead, has ever had the ability to make one?

A pencil has only six component parts: wood, graphite, clay, aluminum, rubber, and paint. But consider what making a pencil by yourself, *from scratch*, would entail. The same set of hands would have to create every one of the six elements, completely and totally.

The first item, wood, seems simple enough. Almost anyone can cut some wood. But if the pencil is truly to be made from scratch, how is the wood to be cut? Tools would be required, and those would also have to be fashioned from scratch. Once cut down, the wood would have to be finely shaped, requiring more tools.

Then the wood would have to be hollowed and filled with graphite, which would have to be mined, mixed with clay, heated at an extremely high temperature, and formed.

There was a time when pencil erasers were made from natural rubber, which would involve extracting latex from rubber trees, then filtering, washing, and combining that latex with acid, and undertaking further processes to finish the rubber. Today, synthetic rubbers are used to make pencil erasers. These are a lot more complicated to produce than natural rubber.

The ferrule, the piece of aluminum that binds the eraser to the wood shaft, and the paint remain. These are not all that easy to make either.

Yet pencils exist. How? The process involves countless people who each do their small part in the production process. From woodcutters to metal smelters to paint makers, a host of people do what they do well, in the places where their skills are valuable. Woodcutters do not work in cities, and metal makers do not ply their craft on mountaintops. So trucks, trains, and planes bring materials from one place to the next, involving still more people in the process.

After the pencils are produced, still more people package them, transport them to stores, and display and sell them.

By the time you buy a pencil, many thousands of people have been involved. And what does it cost to buy a product that has required the efforts of so many people? About fifteen cents.

Leonard Read might have been on to something.

## I, Toaster? I, Sandwich?

None of this is peculiar to pencils, of course, as Thomas Thwaites and Andy George prove.

Thwaites, a designer from the United Kingdom, decided that he would make a toaster from scratch. He was immediately dismayed when, upon taking apart a $10 toaster, he found some four hundred component parts, from copper wire to the plastic housing. Nonetheless, he soldiered on in his attempt to make a toaster all by himself. It took him nine months—and his toaster worked for all of five seconds before it caught fire.

And the toaster was ugly. Thwaites was committed to fashioning his appliance with a plastic housing, but as it turns out, making and molding plastic from scratch is no easy thing. No part of the making of a toaster was easy, nor was it possible to complete any of the steps without cheating. Said Thwaites: "I realise I cheated quite a lot! Though I really did naively set out with the intention of only using pre-industrial tools and methods, I soon realised that...it was impossible."[1] The project proved prohibitively expensive, too, costing $2,360.

Andy George was no less ambitious in wanting to make a sandwich from scratch. He grew his own wheat and vegetables, killed and processed his own chicken (with some help), made his own butter, and harvested his own honey. But like Thwaites, George "cheated" in some respects. He used all kinds of tools and implements in processing his wheat into flour, made use of someone else's beekeeping operation, used preexisting tools and implements in making his butter, and even found an adult chicken to use. All told, it took George six months to make a sandwich. The cost? About $1,500.

Andy George undoubtedly realized what Thomas Thwaites said about making his toaster: "By taking things like trains, or using Wikipedia, or even not making my own shoes for walking to a mine, I was already in a sense 'cheating.'" But cheating is perhaps the least charitable way of characterizing what happens when anyone makes anything. Each human being stands on the shoulders of everyone who has come before, and alongside everyone presently involved in markets. This connectedness is what makes possible the production and delivery of every product we use.

## Unintended Consequences

So in looking into happiness, cooperation, and coercion, we have gone from Socrates to pencils, toasters, and sandwiches. Why?

The answer to that question is relatively straightforward: to understand what is actually possible in terms of governance, we need to understand what is possible for human beings generally. And from Socrates to sandwiches, it should be pretty clear that human beings think they are capable of a great deal more than they are. This affects how we live together in all sorts of ways.

Consider three words that seem always to go together: *health*, *education*, and *welfare*. If no one person, or even any small collection of people, can make something as simple as a pencil, how can a politician, or even a Congressional committee and a phalanx of bureaucrats, hope to deliver something as complex as Americans' health, education, and welfare programs? The important question is to what degree human life can be centrally planned, rather than left to emerge spontaneously, and to what degree it should be.

The fact is that much more of life in the United States is centrally planned than it used to be. The *Code of Federal Regulations* is the published version of the regulations the federal government imposes on the nation.[2] These regulations are, in sum, the federal government's attempt to plan the political, social, and economic life of the nation centrally. They concern everything from space travel to restrictions on pets in public parks. The first year the *Code of Federal Regulations* appeared, 1938, it contained 18,193 pages. At the end of 2017, it contained 186,374 pages. Life became quite a bit more complicated in seventy-nine years.

Few people, none of them sane, would argue in favor of everything being centrally planned. About the same number would argue for nothing being planned at all. So the best answer lies somewhere between 0 and 100 percent, but how far toward one end or the other is it? There is never a clear answer to this question, and reasonable answers will vary over time, place, and circumstance. But there are some things to keep in mind as we think about how much government can be expected to accomplish.

The knowledge problem exists whenever human beings attempt to do anything that is in any way complicated by the needs, desires, and abilities of others. This is especially true when we attempt to use government to achieve our goals, because government decision-makers are typically far removed from the people for whom they make decisions. In light of the knowledge problem, we should be skeptical of what government can achieve.

Such skepticism should grow even stronger because of a byproduct of the knowledge problem: unintended consequences.

Unintended consequences are outcomes that decision-makers didn't intend but that arose as a direct consequence of the decisions they made. Consider, for example, how Australia and New Zealand introduced rabbits into their midst to provide a new food source. Little did anyone know at the time that the rabbit population would proliferate, becoming destructive pests whose drawbacks far outweighed their benefits.

Unintended consequences are not necessarily harmful, and indeed are often quite beneficial. Consider how many drugs turn out to have beneficial effects beyond their intended usage. Aspirin, for example, has proved to be an effective anticoagulant that reduces the risk of heart attacks and mitigates the effects of strokes. The people who created aspirin didn't intend for the drug to do these things, but it does.

Another kind of unintended consequence brings with it perverse results—outcomes that are the exact opposite of what the decision-maker intended. In 2013 the singer and actress Barbra Streisand took exception to pictures of her home being published online, so she sued the publisher. Prior to her filing the lawsuit, only six people had downloaded the photographs of her home, and two of them were her own attorneys. After her lawsuit drew attention to the matter, 420,000 people downloaded the pictures in the following month alone. The episode became so noteworthy that this sort of thing has become known as the "Streisand effect."

Unintended consequences arise both when individuals make decisions for themselves and when politicians and bureaucrats make decisions for them. Government action tends to address complex and weighty issues that affect many people, and the more complicated things get, the more likely unintended consequences are to emerge. And the more weighty the issue being addressed, the more weighty will be the unintended consequences.

## Snakes and Rats

Some examples of the unintended consequences of government action are sadly amusing. There is a legend that when the British ruled India, they attempted to reduce the number of cobras in the streets by offering a bounty on every cobra killed and turned in to authorities.[3] The scheme worked well—so well that cobras became hard to find and enterprising people began raising cobras in their homes to turn in for the bounty. Over time, the authorities realized that although people were continuing to collect bounties, the cobra population was under control. Seeing no point in paying to solve a problem that no longer existed, they discontinued the program. What happened to the now-valueless cobras people were raising in their homes? They released them into the streets, which resulted in a bigger cobra problem than had existed in the first place. This legend has given rise to the term *cobra effect* to refer to a perverse outcome.

Whether the cobra story actually occurred is unclear. But what is clear is that a similar thing did happen in Hanoi during the French colonial period.[4] There the problem was rats. The French authorities offered a bounty for every rat killed but required only that people bring the rats' tails as evidence to collect the reward. Not surprisingly, Hanoi was soon overrun by tailless rats. The people were simply catching the rats, cutting off their tails, and releasing them. Why? So those rats could procreate, creating more rats and more bounties. In the end, Hanoi had more rats after the bounty than before.

Sometimes the perverse outcomes of a policy are not seen as easily, and sometimes the examples are not nearly as amusing. The federal government started requiring seat belts as standard equipment in automobiles in 1968, and forty-nine states now mandate seat belt use for all or some occupants of moving automobiles. Motor vehicle fatalities have decreased, and it seems clear that seat belt use is responsible for at least some of the decline.

But there is more to the story. Seat belt use protects people inside the cars but does little for people outside of them. As more drivers used seat belts, fatalities for pedestrians and cyclists increased.[5]

Why?

As seat belt use rose, driving became safer. As driving became safer, the cost to drivers of being inattentive fell. And as the cost of being inattentive fell, drivers could afford to exercise less care.

> A law specifically designed to help the disabled in the labor market resulted in decreased employment rates for the disabled

Now, many people have an intuition that safety measures would not make them drive any less carefully, an intuition economist Gordon Tullock sought to disprove through a thought experiment. Imagine you are driving a car that has a sharp spike mounted on the steering wheel, aimed directly at your heart. Would you exercise extra care when driving this car compared to driving a typical car? The usual answer is yes. And that's the proof. The more dangerous a car is, the more care a driver will tend to exercise when driving that car. That's the same as saying that the less dangerous a car is, the less care a driver will tend to exercise when driving that car.

So as safety regulations make drivers safer, pedestrians and cyclists face greater risk. An extreme demonstration of this risk occurred in Arizona in 2018. Rafaela Vasquez was the "safety driver" for a self-driving car that Uber was testing.[6] Cutting-edge technology enabled the self-driving car to steer, brake, accelerate, and generally move through traffic the same way a human driver would. Vasquez felt so safe, in fact, that she watched a show on her phone while the car sped down the road. And she was safe. But Elaine Herzberg, a pedestrian pushing a bicycle across four lanes of traffic, was not. An apparent software bug caused the self-driving car to fail to see Herzberg. The car struck and killed her. Although the software bug was the immediate cause of the accident, Vasquez probably could have prevented the accident had she been paying closer attention. The technology made her feel safe enough to exercise less care than she should have.

## The Americans with Disabilities Act

In 1990, the U.S. government enacted the Americans with Disabilities Act. This law attempted to protect the disabled in the labor market by prohibiting discriminatory behavior on the basis of disability, just as legislation had previously outlawed employment discrimination on the basis of race, religion, sex, and other personal characteristics. While much of the law concerns the conditions under which employees can be fired, the law also required employers to provide "reasonable accommodations" for disabled workers. In an effort to avoid unintended consequences, the law excluded from the list of covered disabilities any number of conditions, including pedophilia, kleptomania, and exhibitionism. But that wasn't enough to stave off the perverse outcomes that followed.

A law specifically designed to ensure that the disabled got a fair shake in the labor market instead resulted in decreased employment rates for the disabled.[7] Why? There are a couple of reasons.

First, the law made it expensive for businesses to hire the disabled. The phrase "reasonable accommodation" is open to interpretation, but over the years regulators have deemed it to mean, among other things, that employers might need to modify an employee's physical environment, offer the employee additional training, give him extra time to complete tasks, and even hire interpreters. If an employee's physical condition deteriorates, the employer may be required to give that employee a completely different job that conforms better to his physical condition. All these things increase the cost of doing business.

Second, the law made it difficult to terminate disabled workers, even when warranted. The law forbade employers from terminating disabled workers because of their disabilities. But how is a business to prove that it terminated a disabled worker because of something other than the worker's disability?

The answer that many businesses seem to have arrived at, although few will admit it, is not to hire the disabled in the first place. It turns out to be easier for an employer to prove that it did not hire a disabled worker for a reason unrelated to the worker's disability than to prove that it fired the worker for such a reason. Consequently, the Americans with Disabilities Act actually led to a decrease in employment rates for the disabled. The law had exactly the opposite effect that lawmakers intended.

## Hoy No Circula

Mexico City has terrible air pollution. To address the problem, politicians came up with a plan, called *Hoy No Circula* ("today [your car] does not circulate"), to take 20 percent of the city's cars off the roads every weekday. This simple scheme used the final digit of a vehicle's license plate to disallow certain cars from being on the road on certain days.

But the program didn't improve air quality. In fact, the air quality in Mexico City worsened.[8]

This is because the law caused Mexico City residents to behave in ways that lawmakers failed to anticipate. People who were not allowed to drive their cars on prohibited days none-theless had to get to work. What did many of them do? They bought second cars. And when the law forces someone to buy a second car that he doesn't need and otherwise would not have bought, what sort of car is the person likely to buy? An inexpensive, older car. And the inexpensive, older cars tended to be less environmentally friendly than the cars people had been driving but now couldn't. So the law designed to reduce automobile pollution actually caused automobile pollution to rise.

## Venezuela's Downward Spiral

Perhaps nothing illustrates the problems of unintended consequences better than a series of events that occurred in Venezuela beginning in 1976. On January 1 of that year, Venezuela nationalized the oil industry within its borders, bringing it under the full control of the national government. Politics replaced the profit motive.

The profit motive encourages business owners to maintain physical assets so they can continue earning profits for years to come. Conversely, political motives tend to favor short-term gains and cronyism. So when the Venezuelan government nationalized the oil industry, politicians and bureaucrats neglected to maintain the physical assets needed to extract oil from the ground and refine it. The physical capital deteriorated. That deterioration led to reduced oil production. Reduced oil production led to reduced revenues from oil sales. Reduced oil revenue meant that the government started to find itself short of cash. The cash crunch was an unintended consequence of nationalizing the oil industry.

To address its cash crunch, the Venezuelan government printed money, which gave birth to a number of further unintended consequences. Chief among these was rampant inflation. Depending on whom you ask, Venezuela's annual inflation rate exceeded something between 60,000 percent and 200,000 percent in 2019.[9]

To put that in perspective, a product that cost one dollar in January 2019 would cost between $600 and $2,000 by the end of 2019. So the inflation Venezuela experienced in just twelve months was more than twenty times the inflation the United States experienced over its first 243 years—combined.

This inflation meant, among other things, that people could no longer afford food. What did the government do in response? It regulated the prices that farmers could charge for their products. This had the unintended consequence of preventing farmers from selling their products for a profit, which had the further unintended consequence of halting the farmers' food production. When food production stopped, the government acted yet again, forcing people to work on farms.[10]

Stripped of all nonessential storylines, the Venezuela drama comes down to this: the government enslaved its people as a direct result of its nationalization of the oil industry.

## The Knowledge Problem and Organizing Humans

Let us return to the knowledge problem to see how it connects with unintended consequences.

We know that no one person has enough knowledge even to make a pencil, or a toaster, or a sandwich. We also know that when human beings attempt to direct human affairs too closely, any number of unintended consequences emerge. But in the end, we still make pencils. They cost about fifteen cents. And we make toasters. They cost about twenty-five dollars. And we make sandwiches. They cost about five dollars. Collectively, we not only can do more things than we can individually but also can do those things at a fraction of the cost.

So which is it? Does the knowledge problem mean that collective action invites unintended consequences, or is collective action the key to overcoming the knowledge problem?

The answer lies in how we organize our collective actions. Human beings can and do accomplish astonishing things. They just typically happen in a way that we tend to underappreciate, largely because we cannot see how they happen. The Nobel laureate Friedrich Hayek addressed this issue when he wrote:

> The curious task of economics is to demonstrate to men how little they really know about what they imagine they can design. To the naive mind that can conceive of order only as the product of deliberate arrangement, it may seem absurd that in complex conditions order, and adaptation to the unknown, can be achieved more effectively by decentralizing decisions and that a division of authority will actually extend the possibility of overall order. Yet that decentralization actually leads to more information being taken into account.[11]

When Hayek talks about decentralized decision-making, he is talking about the organizing principle of cooperation. Rather than being directed by a coercive authority, each person makes decisions for himself. It is not that people become disconnected individuals. It is that people become free to form and dissolve associations with one another, and to create and modify rules for their mutual interactions as they cooperate in pursuing their goals. Decentralization of decision-making allows for cooperation, and cooperation allows for "spontaneous orders" to emerge.

Spontaneous orders are systems that develop organically. They aren't designed by a coercive authority. They emerge through countless human interactions undertaken over time. Examples of successful spontaneous orders often go unnoticed because they are all around us.

Consider what happened in Nicaragua with a group of deaf children beginning in 1981. That year, a new school for the deaf opened. Prior to that, most deaf people stayed at home and had little contact with other deaf people. Fifty students enrolled during the school's first year, and a curious thing happened: they developed their own version of sign language. No one taught them this; they simply began assigning signs and gestures to the things in their environment, and slowly a language emerged.

The language evolved over time, the way languages do, until it had a sufficient vocabulary, complete with verb tenses and the like, to rival any other language. There are at present some three thousand speakers of Nicaraguan Sign Language, and the language continues to evolve.[12]

Lest there be any doubt that languages evolve, look at English. Any high school student knows what "twerking," "420," and "YouTuber" mean. What do those words have in common? They were all recently added to the *Oxford English Dictionary*. That older people might not know what any of them means does not stop the English language from evolving.

There are countless other examples of spontaneous order. Could one person have written what we commonly refer to as "the law"? Of course not. The law is an amalgamation of many different kinds of law: municipal codes, county law, state law, federal law, constitutional law. And each of these major divisions has multiple subdivisions.

The internet is perhaps an even simpler example. Markets, and economies more generally, are pretty easy to see, too. Watching people walk through a park even gives evidence of spontaneous order. All one need do is look at where people have worn paths into the grass.

Elements of spontaneous order appear just about everywhere there are human beings. The characteristic that they all share is that they could not have emerged from the mind of one person or even from a small group of people.

## Two Organizing Principles

Which brings us back to our two organizing principles: cooperation and coercion. Given the knowledge problem and unintended consequences, it makes a massive difference whether people choose to organize themselves according to one, the other, or a combination of the two principles.

We can attempt to use coercion to force humans to produce the things we need and behave the way we want, or we can allow spontaneous orders to emerge over time and trust that cooperation will yield the things we need and the behaviors we want.

> **People don't respond to laws. People respond to *incentives*.**

Neither option is perfect. Coercion suffers from the knowledge problem, and cooperation disallows all manner of imposed planning. It would be foolish to suggest that either principle, alone, would answer every problem that human beings face.

These days, people tend to think in terms of coercion. It is easy to imagine what the world would look like if people just did what we told them to do. We want kids to be healthier, so we imagine banning sugary drinks in schools. We want people to drive more slowly along a stretch of road, so we imagine lowering the speed limit.

The problem is that imagining outcomes ignores the fact that people don't respond to laws. People respond to *incentives*. We can try to adjust those incentives by imposing penalties for disobeying laws, but penalties matter only if the lawbreaker is caught and successfully prosecuted. Even then, the incentive to avoid the penalty must be greater than the incentive to disobey the law. Part of the reason that almost thirty million Americans remain uninsured even after the Affordable Care Act established a fine for being uninsured is that the cost of the fine is less than the cost of purchasing insurance.[13] Finally, as numerous examples of unintended consequences demonstrate, even if we coerce people into altering their behaviors, we may end up causing them to do other things we like even less.

The importance of incentives helps explain why choosing the appropriate organizing principle matters so much: incentives change dramatically depending on whether people are operating in a cooperative model or under a coercive authority. The key to making people's lives better is knowing when coercion will work and when it would be best to leave people alone to cooperate. Given the complicated nature of human life, it should come as no surprise that this is not a simple binary choice.

# 2

# RIGHTS AND WRONGS

After living through the dark days of prohibition in Springfield, Homer Simpson held his glass high and offered a toast: "To alcohol, the cause of, and solution to, all of life's problems."[1] In many respects, Homer's take on alcohol is what Americans *should* think about rights; they are both the cause of and solution to most of our political problems.

This starts to become clear when we consider the relative merits of cooperation and coercion, and how these two things play out in our daily lives. At some point in our history we decided that the coercive power of government should be used to achieve good outcomes rather than merely to prevent bad ones. This newfound optimism regarding what government could be expected to accomplish replaced the previous, more pessimistic view, which understood government to be a necessary but dangerous thing. In short, we traded in Tom Paine and Thomas Jefferson for FDR. That shift played out slowly over generations.

And as it did, our understanding of rights changed, too, resulting in any number of unintended consequences.

## What Are Rights?

An examination of the history of rights in the United States reveals a massive shift in the language we use. The word *rights* now encompasses far more than it did earlier in our history. The thoroughgoing expansion of the term's meaning has caused us to lose sight of why rights were central to the American experiment in the first place, and of the role they were supposed to play in our political life.

By the time Thomas Jefferson wrote the Declaration of Independence in 1776, the word *rights* was in the American vernacular. This was due, in no small part, to the hostilities with Great Britain. In Jefferson's time and for a while beyond, the concept of a right was straightforward: a right was a part of human life that lay outside of government control. To define a right was to create a zone of noninterference for citizens where their government was concerned.

The sense of noninterference was so ingrained that Alexander Hamilton, in *Federalist* 84, argued against including a Bill of Rights in the Constitution because people might misinterpret its presence to imply that the Constitution defined what the government may not do rather than what it may do. It turns out that Hamilton's concern was well placed. Today, many people, including many elected officials, regard the Bill of Rights as a list of freedoms that government grants to the people rather than as a list of restrictions people impose on government.

In the Declaration, Jefferson introduced the idea of rights by discussing their origins and nature rather than by offering an exhaustive list of what they included. He famously wrote,

"We hold these truths to be self-evident, that all men are created equal, that they are endowed by their Creator with certain unalienable Rights, that among these are Life, Liberty and the pursuit of Happiness."

Following this, he explained the proper role of government, which was nothing other than to secure the rights of individuals:

> That to secure these rights, Governments are instituted among Men, deriving their just powers from the consent of the governed,—That whenever any Form of Government becomes destructive of these ends, it is the Right of the People to alter or to abolish it, and to institute new Government, laying its foundation on such principles and organizing its powers in such form, as to them shall seem most likely to effect their Safety and Happiness.

In the Jeffersonian formulation, rights are both *natural* and *negative*. Natural rights are rights people have by virtue of their humanity. Because natural rights arise from our nature as humans, they precede government and render humans fundamentally equal. When governments enact laws to treat people equally under the law, they are not bestowing equality; they are recognizing it. As Jefferson said elsewhere, "The mass of mankind has not been born with saddles on their backs, nor a favored few booted and spurred, ready to ride them legitimately, by the grace of God."[2] No one can lay claim to the right of ruling, and all enjoy the same fundamental rights.

**The shift in our conception of rights has led to a virtually limitless federal government**

Because natural rights all stand athwart governmental intrusion into the private sphere, they are relatively easy to name.

Most Americans list them when asked what rights they have, and at least some of them appear in the Bill of Rights, which was ratified in 1791.

These sorts of rights—like the rights to free speech, to freedom of religion, to keep and bear arms, and to freedom of the press—protect Americans not from one another but from their government. One can exercise these rights without making any claim against other citizens. Sure, it may be irritating to listen to your neighbor exercise his right to free speech, and you might worry if he exercises his right to keep and bear arms, but these rights do not require some citizens to pay a subsidy for others to enjoy their rights.

So in addition to being natural rights, they are also *negative* rights. The most common formulation to explain such rights is that they provide "freedom from" governmental intervention.

The word *negative* contains no pejorative element here, just as there is nothing pejorative about referring to the negative pole on a battery. But the existence of negative rights points to the possibility of a different kind of rights—positive rights.

Where negative rights are "freedom from" rights, positive rights are typically described as "freedom to" rights. We hear about these kinds of rights all the time in today's political discourse. How often do you hear politicians and pundits declare that every American should have a right to healthcare, or a college education, or even an income?

Positive rights are an entirely different animal from negative rights. If you have the right *to* something, that places a duty on others to provide it. And unlike negative rights, positive rights do not disempower the government in the least. In fact, they enable, even require, government to do all sorts of things, typically in the name of enhancing the welfare of the citizenry.

It is in the difference between these two kinds of rights that we find the fundamental friction of American political life. On one hand, the nation was founded on a set of rights that disallows the government from doing things. On the other, we find citizens calling for a set of rights that *requires* the government to do things. And the things the government must do in pursuance of positive rights violate people's negative rights.

Consider the negative right of owning property. By working, people earn money. That is their property. The government has no right to take their property except through taxation, which is then used to address common needs, things like federal courthouses, post offices, and the military—things that the federal government is constitutionally empowered to provide.

In an environment of negative rights, a limited government necessarily results. But in an environment of positive rights, a very large and powerful government emerges. Look at the drivers of big government over the past several decades and you'll find many programs set up to deliver on positive rights, including Social Security, Medicare, Medicaid, and the Affordable Care Act. Such programs have fundamentally changed both the nature of American government and what citizens expect government to accomplish.

The shift in our conception of rights from the negative to the positive has led to a federal government that is virtually limitless in what it attempts.

## Reconciling Negative and Positive Rights

Can negative and positive rights coexist? The short answer to this question is no, because every advance in positive rights diminishes negative rights, if only in terms of property rights. But the long answer is more complex, and more interesting.

The United States, from its earliest history, has tried to reconcile negative and positive formulations of rights, and it has had

quite a bit of success in doing so. While Thomas Jefferson supported limited government and negative rights, he also supported
public education, which means that he perceived education to be
a positive right. Someone must pay for schools, and a hallmark of
positive rights is the need for some to pay the cost for others. Jefferson's proposed 1779 legislation, "A Bill for the More General
Diffusion of Knowledge," was quite limited in scope compared
to what we now do in the name of public education—it was to
provide only three years of tax-funded schooling for "all the free
children, male and female." Nonetheless, it illustrates that, right
from the beginning, Americans struggled with the question of
just how much government should attempt to accomplish.

The desire for positive rights emerged early in American history, but it took a fair amount of time before this desire over-
took Americans' commitment to negative rights. At some point,
though, enough voters decided that government was less a thing
to be frightened of than a tool with which they might accomplish
all manner of good. To get a good deal more in terms of positive
rights than the minimal version they had previously experienced,
the people had to give up their negative rights to some degree.

Put another way, the potential for cooperation among people
had to give way to a greater level of coercion.

This shift in political thought makes perfect sense in the
context of history. People understandably wanted certain guarantees in their lives, be it in the form of guaranteed healthcare,
housing, or some other desired outcome. Cooperation, after all,
doesn't guarantee outcomes; it simply creates a context within
which good things that people want might emerge. What are
we to do when these things do not emerge, or do not emerge in
sufficient quantity for everyone to enjoy? Coercion can, to some
degree, offer a guarantee of results.

The people's desire for a "full implementation" of the positive rights regime had become evident by 1944, when President

Franklin Roosevelt offered a new vision to the American people in that year's State of the Union address. Roosevelt offered what has come to be known as the Second, or Economic, Bill of Rights. To push his economic plan, Roosevelt co-opted the language of the Bill of Rights. But where the Bill of Rights almost exclusively protected negative rights by enumerating things the government may not do to people, Roosevelt's Second Bill of Rights entrenched positive rights by describing things the government should do for people. Roosevelt's list:

- The right to a useful and remunerative job in the industries, or shops or farms or mines of the Nation;
- The right to earn enough to provide adequate food and clothing and recreation;
- The right of every farmer to raise and sell his products at a return which will give him and his family a decent living;
- The right of every businessman, large and small, to trade in an atmosphere of freedom from unfair competition and domination by monopolies at home or abroad;
- The right of every family to a decent home;
- The right to adequate medical care and the opportunity to achieve and enjoy good health;
- The right to adequate protection from the economic fears of old age, sickness, accident, and unemployment;
- The right to a good education.

Everyone might agree that these are good things and that the world would be wonderful if everyone had them. But to categorize these as "rights" is to claim that the government should use coercive force to take from some people whatever is needed to supply these things to others.

Something had clearly flowered by 1944. The positive rights

FDR listed inspired politicians to bring into being any number
of federal programs. Social Security, Medicare, Medicaid, the
Affordable Care Act, and Unemployment Insurance, along with
a host of smaller programs, are direct outgrowths of the change
in America's political orientation toward positive rights.

The scope of this change is clear in the data. Government
spending as a fraction of all spending in the economy reveals the
magnitude of the government's role in the economy. Since 1792,
there have been three periods in U.S. history when government
spending rose precipitously: the Civil War, World War I, and
World War II. In each case, government spending, as a fraction of all spending in the economy, jumped between five- and
eightfold for the duration of the war.

To get a clearer picture of the expansion of government over
time, we can remove the wars to reveal a more general trend.

From 1792 until 1928—a period of more than 130 years—
federal government spending remained relatively stable at about

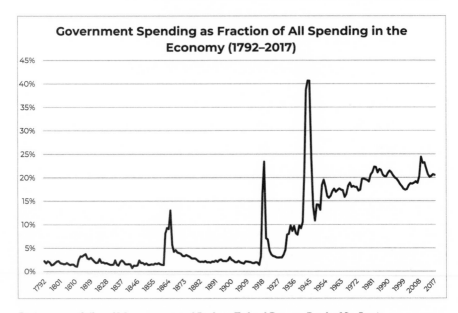

*Data sources: Office of Management and Budget, Federal Reserve Bank of St. Louis*

2.5 percent of all spending in the economy. But from just before the time that Franklin Roosevelt became president in 1932, government spending began to grow—from less than 3 percent of the economy prior to 1928, to 10 percent in the 1930s, to 17 percent in the 1950s, to 22 percent today. The growth of government spending has happened as a direct result of the expansion of positive rights and the government apparatus necessary to implement those rights.

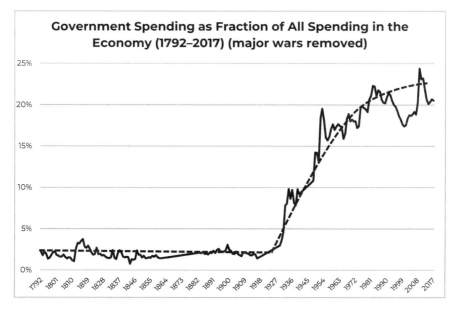

*Data sources: Office of Management and Budget, Federal Reserve Bank of St. Louis*

We can turn away from economic measures and still see this phenomenon. Consider the *Code of Federal Regulations*, the compendium of all the federal government's regulations on American citizens and others living within U.S. borders. When first published—not surprisingly, also in the 1930s—the *Code* contained about 18,000 pages of printed regulations, which seemed quite a lot at the time. Now there are almost 200,000 pages.

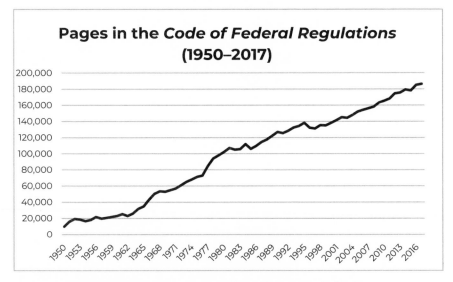

**Pages in the *Code of Federal Regulations* (1950–2017)**

*Data sources: Office of Management and Budget, Federal Reserve Bank of St. Louis*

The political reality is that it is impossible to guarantee every-one housing, food, clothing, and all the other things Roosevelt listed in his Second Bill of Rights without also denying those same people their freedom and the rights that flow from it.

The economic reality, bleaker still, is that it is simply impos-sible to guarantee these things at all. In the end, the price for more positive rights is fewer negative rights.

The curious thing is that we called into question what coop-eration could accomplish but never asked what government could accomplish. The possibilities of what cooperation can yield are limited, as all human endeavors are. Why, then, do we not as readily consider the limitations of what coercion can yield? For public policies to work as promised often requires that economic realities and limitations be ignored. But we ignore them at our peril.

The federal debt, massive and growing, seems a clear indi-cation that for far too long we have ignored what is possible in favor of what is desirable.

# 3

# THE MAGIC WAND

People have become conditioned to turn to government and say, "Fix this."

This is what happens when a people's desire for positive rights overtakes their dedication to negative rights. To say that someone has a positive right to a thing is also to say that other people have a corresponding duty to provide that thing when any cooperative effort falls short. So growing coercion *always* accompanies the growth of positive rights.

In their zeal to attain things they want, people have come to regard government as a magic wand of sorts, capable of achieving practically anything.

Franklin Roosevelt's Second Bill of Rights declared that all people have a "right to a useful and remunerative job."[1] But how can this possibly be the case? Business owners hire the employees they require based on what consumers want and are willing to pay, and how productive the workers are. What if there are unemployed people no employer needs? The government could levy fines on businesses for not hiring these people, but that wouldn't create useful jobs, merely busywork. To say that a person has a right to a useful and remunerative job is to ignore what that person has the skills and will to do and the extent to which other people value what that person does.

The belief that government can alter these realities to achieve a goal is magic-wand thinking. Directing government to coerce an outcome into existence does not, in fact, mean that the outcome will emerge. Whatever human limitations prevented people from achieving an outcome by cooperation might well also prevent them from achieving that outcome by coercion.

The faith that people unthinkingly place in government to accomplish goals is at the same time a faith in the people who work in government, so-called public servants. But people who work in government are no more knowledgeable, capable, motivated, or well intentioned than their counterparts outside of government. Humans who work in government are the very same kinds of humans as those who don't, and they are subject to all the same motivations as everyone else. So many people miss this fundamental point in so many ways that it is mind-boggling.

The failure to recognize this basic truth becomes painfully clear nearly every time someone identifies a problem he would like to address, be it the need for a living wage, affordable housing, or medical care. Almost invariably, government emerges as the supposed solution to the problem. But what people imagine will happen and what actually happens when we ask government to fix a problem are rarely, if ever, the same thing. To see why, consider the three broad groups of people involved: voters, politicians, and bureaucrats.

People typically imagine that the voters' goal is to advocate beneficial laws, and that the way they do this is by voting for politicians who support the sorts of legislation the voters favor.

People typically imagine that the politicians' goal is to do what's in the best interest of society, and that the way they do this is to design and vote for effective laws of the type the voters want. People typically imagine that the bureaucrats' goal is to serve the public, and that the way they do this is by executing the laws to the ends that the legislators intended.

But none of this comports with what we understand about human behavior.

The goals of the voter, the politician, and the bureaucrat are all the same, because each is a human being and all human beings have the same ultimate goal: to maximize their own happiness. The way the voter maximizes his happiness is to become informed and to vote if he expects that the benefit from doing so will exceed the cost. The way the politician maximizes his happiness is to convince at least half of the people who choose to vote to vote for him. The way the bureaucrat maximizes his happiness is to craft his job to satisfy his needs. Although this runs counter to the popular imagination, it all becomes pretty clear, pretty quickly, under even the weakest of microscopes.

**What people imagine will happen and what actually happens when we ask government to fix a problem are rarely, if ever, the same thing**

## Voters

All human beings seek to maximize their happiness. Voters are human beings. Therefore, voters seek to maximize their happiness. That's what they do, because that's what everyone does. But how? A simple thought experiment tells the tale.

Imagine a society composed of a hundred people: ninety in group A, and the remaining ten in group B. These hundred people are considering a proposed law that will have the government take $10 from each person in group A, burn half of the money, and divide what's left among the people in group B. What happens if this proposed law is enacted? The ninety people in group A will each pay $10, for a total of $900. Burning half of it leaves $450 to be divided among the ten people in group B, giving each person in group B $45. The people in group B will clearly favor this proposal and will vote for it. The people in group A, however, will see no wisdom in this legislation and will vote it down handily. In any rational world, this legislation will be defeated 90–10, and everyone will move on to other, hopefully more reasonable, things.

This is how we imagine that voter behavior works in a democracy, and although it gets the big picture right, it misses where details are concerned. The most important detail missing here is that voting isn't costless. In terms of money, time, effort, aggravation, or a combination of all four, it costs something to vote. First, a voter has to pay attention to what laws are proposed. He then has to read the proposed law. Next, he has to think about whether what the law proposes is good and reasonable, and decide which way to vote. Finally, he has to go to the voting place, cast a vote, and return home. This means that he also has to pay attention to and think carefully about issues, candidates, and elections. He has to assess what proposed laws will cost generally, and what they might cost him personally. He has to assess whether he thinks political candidates are even telling the truth.

In short, there is not one simple cost. There are a number of them. And they add up.

In our thought experiment, we can simulate all of these costs with a fee. Consider the same proposed law: The government will take $10 from each of the ninety people in group A, burn half of the money, and divide what's left among the ten people in group B. But this time, there is a $20 fee to vote. What happens when this proposal is put to the vote? Each person in group B still stands to gain $45 if the proposed law is passed. That's more than the $20 voting fee, so the people in group B have an incentive to vote for the proposal. But what of the people in group A? If the proposal passes, each person in group A will have to pay $10. But since it costs $20 to vote, the people in group A are actually better off not voting. For a person in group A, the cost of living with the new law is lower than the cost of voting against it. Not only will the law pass under these circumstances, it will pass unanimously, 10–0.

All of this is more complicated in the real world, of course, but the complexities merely add noise to the underlying reality.[2] The underlying reality is that, in a democracy, laws are not enacted based on whether they are good for society. They are enacted based on whether they benefit or harm the people who have an incentive to vote. As a result, laws that impose on society a greater cost than benefit often pass. They do so when the benefit is concentrated in the hands of a small group of people and the cost is spread over a large one. This is the principle of concentrated benefits and dispersed costs. And this principle results in all kinds of legislative mischief.

In 2015, Phoenix voters were asked to vote on a proposal to increase the city's sales tax by 0.3 percentage points in order to raise more than $30 billion to build and maintain twenty-six miles of light rail in the city.[3] The plan also included laying 680 miles of asphalt, creating 1,080 miles of bike lanes, and adding 135 miles of sidewalks. In addition, the City Council voted that if the proposal passed, the City Council would shift $16 million annually from the transit budget to the city police budget.

From the money citizens spent on advertising trying to influence voters, it appears that people overwhelmingly supported the plan. In total, citizens spent almost $400,000 advertising in favor of the proposal, and just over $400 advertising against it.

But a different picture emerges on closer examination. That $400,000 came mostly from engineers, contractors, and police—groups that all stood to collect the lion's share of that $30 billion in spending. Meanwhile, the cost of the proposal was spread over the 1.6 million people living in Phoenix. For a family that spends $30,000 a year on goods subject to the tax, a 0.3-percentage-point sales tax boost costs $90 per year—or less than a basic Netflix subscription. For the average voter who did not stand to gain personally from the light rail project, the cost of fighting the project (given all the other daily demands on people's time) wasn't worth it.

Where the outcome of the vote was concerned, the question wasn't whether the light rail project was a good idea for Phoenix voters. What mattered was that it was a great idea for a small group of Phoenix voters and an idea not worth fighting over for almost everyone else. How do we know it wasn't worth fighting over? There are more than 830,000 registered voters in Phoenix.[4] Yet only about 135,000 cast votes on the light rail proposal.[5] Fewer than 20 percent of Phoenix voters bothered to vote on the matter at all. Given the incentives involved, a good portion of that 20 percent probably stood to gain personally from the light rail construction.

The transit proposal passed, 55 percent to 45 percent.

Voters are often criticized for being ignorant or unconcerned. What voters actually are is rationally ignorant. There are any number of things they do not know, and given the various voting and information costs they face, it is perfectly reasonable that they remain ignorant of these things. After all, they have more important things to do, like mowing the lawn, picking up their children from soccer practice, making dinner, and worrying about paying bills. The problem is that, in our idealized way of looking at the political process, we generally assume that voters are something that they are not: concerned with all things in equal measure and ready, willing, and able to act on that concern.

## Politicians

Politicians are also human beings, contrary to what you might hear elsewhere. And human beings seek to maximize their happiness. As with voters, the syllogism holds here, too.

When asked what a politician's goal is, many people idealistically respond, "To do what's in the best interests of society." There are some politicians who truly do seek to do what's in the best interests of society (to the extent that they know what those interests are). But two politicians who are identical in every way except that one's primary goal is to do what's in the best interests of society and the other's is to get elected will experience remarkably different results. The latter will, on average, win more elections, precisely because that is his goal. Economist Thomas Sowell says it more succinctly: "No one will really understand politics until they understand that politicians are not trying to solve our problems. They are trying to solve their own problems—of which getting elected and reelected are number one and number two. Whatever is number three is far behind."[6]

The way politicians get elected (then reelected) is by offering (then appearing to deliver) things the voters want. The problem with this statement is that there is really no such thing as "the voters." There are many individuals who vote, and each of those individuals wants something different.

Consider individual voter preferences for government services, be it healthcare, public schooling, or public transportation. The particular service doesn't really matter, as the same result inevitably emerges. The military provides as good an example as any. Many voters believe that we have no business intervening militarily in other countries. These voters prefer that the government maintain a relatively small and inexpensive military. Many other voters believe the United States should pursue an interventionist foreign policy, part of which includes having a large, well-equipped, and necessarily expensive military. Fewer voters occupy the middle ground between these extremes—a military large enough to be expensive but not large enough to be effective.

In seeking votes, a politician will position himself to attract as many voters as possible. A politician who positions himself as a "dove" will attract the voters who want a small and inexpensive military. A politician who positions himself as a "hawk" will attract the voters who want a large and expensive military.

But what of the minority of voters in the middle who want a moderate-sized, yet ineffectual military? The politician who is closer to the middle will get their votes. So the dovish politician has an incentive to move to be a little less dovish so as to pick up those voters. Then the hawkish politician has an incentive to move to be less hawkish so as to take those voters away from the dove. The dove then has an incentive to become less dovish still to win them back. The politicians play this game until they end up roughly in the middle, with each holding about 50 percent of the vote. In the end, what determines how the election will go is what the minority in the middle want. Carrying the minority center is what makes the difference between winning and losing.

This phenomenon happens with such regularity that it has a name: the *median voter theorem*. The theorem holds that, with majority voting, the median voter's preference will win even if it is the preference of the fewest number of voters.

Consider public education. If you pick an American at random and ask for his opinion about funding for public education, more likely than not he will say that funding for public education is a problem. But you'll get markedly different answers to the follow-up question, "How so?" Many will say we aren't spending enough. Many others will say we are spending too much. The same applies to healthcare, national rail service, and Social Security. About half of polled voters say we should increase the size and scope of these services, and about half say we should cut them. Very few say that they are about the right size.

Politicians seek to win elections not by offering sound public policy that will yield good results but by appealing to 50 percent plus one of the voters. The way they appeal to that many voters is by appealing to the median voter. But the median voter often wants something very different from what people with strong opinions *on either side of an issue* want.

Removing the rose-colored glasses that have us romanticizing politics is the first step to understanding politicians. Politicians seek first to maximize their own happiness, because that's what all humans do.

## Public Bureaucrats

So far, we have seen that neither voters nor politicians act in ways most people assume they do. The group left to consider is public bureaucrats—people who work in government but are not elected. We imagine that public bureaucrats work to serve the public. We go so far as to refer to them as "public servants." But bureaucrats try to craft their jobs to satisfy their needs, because, like the rest of us, they seek to maximize their happiness. Although bureaucrats exist in the public and private sectors, competition forces private-sector bureaucrats (or at least their managers) to focus on satisfying their customers' needs, because they will make no money any other way. Public-sector and private-sector bureaucrats are not intrinsically different; they behave differently only because they face different incentives.

Bureaucracies come in any number of sizes and shapes, but that doesn't seem to have much impact on how they behave. Consider the Department of Veterans Affairs, which exists largely to provide medical benefits for veterans of the U.S. armed forces. The cabinet-level department, formed in 1930, employs more than 375,000 people. Were it not part of the government, it would fit comfortably among the top ten of U.S. employers.

The VA's stated goals are laudable. Providing good medical care to veterans after their years of service is something on which most Americans can agree. So why is it that most people seem to know that the medical care the VA offers is substandard?

> **Government is a powerful tool but not a magic one**

The VA provides substandard care precisely *because* it is a government bureaucracy, and the people who work there face few consequences for placing their own needs above the needs of the people they purportedly serve. Certainly the VA has many dedicated and competent employees. But all it takes is one incompetent or lazy nurse, secretary, or manager to counteract the good done by many competent people. If only 1 percent of VA workers is incompetent, that's almost 4,000 people in positions to create mischief.

How bad have things gotten at the VA? In 2014 it came to light that thousands of patients were backlogged at the Phoenix VA hospital, some of whom died as they waited for care. VA investigators discovered that administrators had been well aware of the problem but had falsified wait-time data in order to collect bonuses.[7] This is perhaps the worst kind of example of bureaucrats' crassly pursuing self-interest at the expense of those they were charged with servicing.

These problems were not local to Arizona. VA administrators all over the country were doing precisely the same thing. A 2016 *USA Today* investigation found that "supervisors instructed employees to falsify patient wait times at VA medical facilities in at least seven states" and that "employees at 40 VA medical facilities in 19 states and Puerto Rico regularly 'zeroed out' veteran wait times."[8]

The people who did these sorts of things were not worthy of the title *public servant*, but we would probably be better off if we dropped that phrase from our lexicon regardless. People serve themselves first, and incentives dictate the rest of their behavior. If this is natural, and it appears for all the world that it is, producing different results requires realigning incentives.

Maybe the VA bureaucracy fails so spectacularly because it is large to the point of being unwieldy. If that is the case, our experience with smaller bureaucracies should yield different outcomes. We should be able to point to any number of state-level bureaucracies that actually satisfy their customers as a rule. Every state in the union has some variant of a Department of Motor Vehicles, and almost every citizen in each of those states will, sooner or later, visit one of those offices. So what do we think about our respective DMVs?

People generally loathe their trips to the DMV. Customers face long wait times. Once to the front of the line, people often learn that they have insufficient documentation in hand, even though they have taken pains to comply with published lists of requirements. All of this is served up by surly clerks who clearly do not concern themselves much with the "customer experience." But why would they? They do not have to.

A trip to any local bureaucratic office yields much the same result, because such outcomes are baked into the system. If human beings seek to maximize their own happiness, then that is what they will do in the face of their incentives and constraints. The incentives and constraints government bureaucrats face do not force them to put anyone else's interests before their own, so those who choose not to simply don't have to.

The story is exactly reversed for business owners. It is uncommon, for example, to see all of the best parking spaces in a store's parking lot reserved for store employees. You might see one set aside for the employee of the month or some such thing, but that tends to be the extent of it. In fact, managers will often ask their employees to park away from the building to keep the spots near the entrance open for customers. But post offices, schools, and municipal buildings? Not so much. Often, the prime parking spots there are reserved for the employees.

This isn't because private-sector workers are more conscientious. Workers in the private sector would love to reserve the spots close to their buildings for themselves. They don't because customers who find the parking inconvenient will take their business elsewhere. The same is not true where government bureaucracies are concerned. Bureaucrats work for government, and government faces no competition. People who work at the post office, as kind and thoughtful as they may be, have less incentive than do workers at the local grocery store to be concerned with customers' having a good experience and coming back. If the U.S. Postal Service cannot earn enough money from customers (as it hasn't for more than a decade), it can turn to the federal government for increased funding.[9] The government, in turn, will coerce the funding from taxpayers. By contrast, a grocery store will just go out of business, to be replaced with one that can serve its customers better.

## Voters, Politicians, and Bureaucrats: A Word of Caution

People attribute almost magical powers to government because they clearly see the outcomes they want to attain—more jobs, less crime, better education—and they clearly see that government has the power to coerce. People imagine that, to achieve X or to prevent Y, all one need do is pass a law requiring people to do X or prohibiting them from doing Y.

But this entire concept is based on a false assumption. Remember, people don't respond to laws; they respond to incentives. This goes for the voters who elect politicians, for the politicians who craft laws, and for the bureaucrats who implement the laws. People are people. Voters have a strong incentive to avoid the cost of becoming informed; politicians, to attract more voters; bureaucrats, to make their jobs less difficult. These incentives explain why empowering government to pursue one outcome often produces a very different outcome. They also explain why the customer experience is so different in public-sector versus private-sector services: the Postal Service versus FedEx, Amtrak versus Southwest, applying for a driver's license versus applying for a credit card, or applying for federal financial aid versus applying for a bank loan.

Government is a powerful tool but not a magic one. And once people realize that unintended outcomes are the rule rather than the exception, they can begin to temper their expectations as to what government can actually achieve. Government cannot accomplish all things, and it is dangerous to believe that it *can* do so. Every sentence that begins with "The government should..." implies the use of coercion. And the coercion that follows is not always worth what it costs, in terms of money, time, emotional distress, or human dignity. The trick is in knowing under what circumstances the reality of what coercion can achieve is more desirable than the reality of what cooperation can achieve.

# PART 2

# COOPERATION AND COERCION IN EVERYDAY LIFE

# 4

# THE MINIMUM WAGE

Remember that first job you had? You were probably sixteen or seventeen years old and doing some menial, entry-level work that bored you to tears. Unless you were one of the lucky few with more marketable skills (like child actors and teen pop stars), you were earning the minimum wage. You were thus the beneficiary of the federal minimum wage law.

Or were you?

The minimum wage is an example of coercion. Many people believe that it is an acceptable application of coercion because the minimum wage protects workers. It guarantees an hourly income, and many people have benefited over the years from this federal wage floor. Many people have earned higher wages than they would have without minimum wage legislation.

But the dirty secret of the minimum wage is that it doesn't help everyone. Any number of people are hurt, and many of them are the same workers the minimum wage is intended to benefit.

The minimum wage does the most harm to two groups of people: low-skill, low-education, low-experience workers—let's call them "marginal workers"—and small business owners. These are the groups that find it hardest to get together in the labor market in the first place, and for similar reasons. Because marginal workers lack valuable job skills, they don't have a lot to offer to prospective employers. Because small business owners lack financial resources, they don't have a lot to offer prospective workers. Marginal workers must compete for jobs against better-skilled, more experienced workers. Small business owners must compete for workers against large companies with far greater financial resources.

And the minimum wage makes it much harder for both groups to compete.

## The Politics of the Minimum Wage

Of course, you would never know the minimum wage hurts anyone by listening to politicians, who reaffirm their love affair with the minimum wage just in time for every election. The rhetoric is always the same.

Take, for example, President Barack Obama's 2013 State of the Union Address, when he said: "Tonight, let's declare that in the wealthiest nation on earth, no one who works full-time should have to live in poverty, and raise the federal minimum wage to $9 an hour. This single step would raise the incomes of millions of working families."[1] But is this the sort of thing one can simply declare? President Obama believed so, and he was by no means alone in this belief. Many Republican politicians also support minimum wage legislation.[2] Most politicians debate what the minimum wage should be, not whether we should have one in the first place. It is a useful political ploy. Politicians declare that workers be paid a certain amount and then leave business owners to figure out where to find the money to pay them.

A wage rate is simply the price of labor, and all prices are determined by supply and demand. To understand the effects of a minimum wage, we need to look at both the demand and the supply of labor, and recognize that the "supply of labor" is really the "supplies of labors," where the supply of marginal workers is separate from the supply of skilled, experienced, and educated workers.

## The Economics of the Minimum Wage

Of course, people aren't commodities, but the laws of supply and demand apply to people's labor just as they apply to commodities. How much an employer is willing to pay to have a job done depends on the value of the completed work to the employer. What is that work worth to the employer? This depends on what it's worth to the employer's customers.

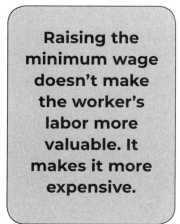

Raising the minimum wage doesn't make the worker's labor more valuable. It makes it more expensive.

Suppose an employer hires workers to wash cars for $7 an hour. If the work is worth $10 to the customer, then it is worth $3 to the employer—because $3 is what will be left after the customer pays the employer and the employer pays the worker.

A $12 minimum wage puts the employer in a tough spot, by requiring him to pay the worker $12 to do a job for which the customer is willing to pay only $10. When the minimum wage causes the cost of a job to exceed the maximum consumers are willing to pay to have it done, the job disappears. Typists are a good example. Until the 1980s, companies employed entire teams of typists. People would handwrite or dictate memos or letters and then hand them over to the "typing pool." Typing was actually a course taught in high schools and business schools. Today, almost 80 percent of American households have computers, and many people teach themselves to type while still children.[3] Consequently, the maximum price people are willing to pay to have someone type for them is often less than the minimum wage. As a matter of fact, it is often $0.

Back to car washes. What happens if the government tells the employer he must pay his worker $9 to wash a car? The customer is willing to pay $10, so that means the job (after the employer pays the worker $9) is worth $1 to the employer. Because $1 is greater than zero, the job won't disappear, right? Not so fast. Owning a business is risky. The employer faces economic downturns, new competitors, changing customer tastes, lawsuits from disgruntled customers or employees, and hundreds of other risks. If the employer cannot earn a large enough profit to compensate him for the risk of owning the business, he will close down and invest his money somewhere less risky, more profitable, or, ideally, both.

And this is where marginal workers and small businesses enter the story. Marginal workers have fewer skills, less education, and less experience than other workers. They can do fewer jobs for which customers are willing to pay.

Consider the story of a small business owner named Brian Choi. He was the owner of a small grocery store in a rough neighborhood in Atlanta.[4] Two kids from the neighborhood, Willie and Maurice Mathews, used to hang around the store's doorstep. They needed money and asked Choi whether they could help out. He turned them down at first, but then he made them a deal. He offered to let them work for tips. Their parents approved the arrangement. The Mathews brothers started by carrying bags for customers, and eventually they ran errands for Choi and even worked the registers. He bought them clothes and gave them cash along the way.

Enter the federal government. When the U.S. Department of Labor discovered that Choi was not paying the Mathews brothers the minimum wage, he was fined $1,500, ordered to pay more than $5,000 in back wages, and threatened with jail time.

The two brothers had no meaningful job skills and no meaningful education, so the most customers were willing to pay for their labor was less than the minimum wage. Choi's small business was fraught with risk—a few years earlier, a robber had shot Choi in the chest. Yet all parties concerned—Choi, the Mathews brothers, and Choi's customers—were willing to engage in the labor market. Though the work wasn't worth the minimum wage, the customers were willing to pay a small amount in exchange for help with their groceries. Though the Mathewses weren't earning the minimum wage, they were willing to accept the small payments in exchange for their time and effort. Though Choi couldn't afford to pay the minimum wage, he was willing to let the brothers work for tips because his customers were happy for the help. If these three groups were free to cooperate, they would do exactly what they were doing before the government stepped in.

Would it have been better for the Mathews brothers to earn the minimum wage, and for the customers to receive work worth the minimum wage, and for Choi to be able to pay the minimum wage? Absolutely. But none of those things was possible. What was possible? The Mathews brothers could hang out on the streets all day earning nothing and providing no value to anyone, or they could participate in this arrangement wherein they, the customers, and Choi benefited.

When the government brought the force of coercion to bear on this cooperative arrangement, Choi had no choice but to pay the government's back-wage claim and then terminate his arrangement with Willie and Maurice Mathews.[5]

In the end, everyone lost. Minimum wage law failed the Mathews brothers, Choi, and Choi's customers because politicians assumed false alternatives. They assumed that the alternative to being paid less than the minimum wage was to be paid the minimum wage. In the brothers' case, being paid the minimum wage was never the alternative. The alternative was not to be paid at all.

This is the human cost of the minimum wage that politicians never talk about.

## The Reality of the Minimum Wage for Employers

Politicians might want everyone who works to make more money, but many jobs simply are not worth more. To get to the bottom of this, you need to think like an employer, which is easy enough. Just think about all the people you *don't hire* to work around your home.

You probably wouldn't pay one of the neighborhood kids $9 an hour to paint your house. Why? Because he has no experience painting houses and you would end up with a $9-an-hour mess. When it comes to painting houses, his labor is not worth $9 an hour. A professional painter's might be, but a typical child's most certainly is not. You probably don't pay someone to wash your clothes at $9 an hour either. Or get your mail. Or sweep your front porch.

Now, you might think, "I don't hire someone to do those things because I can do them myself." But what you're really saying is, "Since I have the time to do those things, it's not worth it for me to pay someone else $9 an hour to do them for me." And that's the point. The primary question isn't whether you can *afford* to pay the wage but whether the person's labor is *worth* the wage to you.

The situation is similar with employers. The relevant question isn't whether the employer can afford to pay more but whether the labor is worth the additional amount the employer must pay. Raising the minimum wage doesn't make the worker's labor more valuable. It only makes it more expensive.

When the minimum wage rises, the employer will view each of his workers as falling into one of two groups—those who are worth the higher wage and those who aren't. The former keep their jobs. The latter are shown the door. People in the first group are a bit better off. People in the second group are far worse off.

It is easy for politicians to put a human face on the benefits of a minimum wage hike. They do this all the time. You can expect to see a minimum wage worker in the Rose Garden ceremony when a President signs legislation increasing the wage. Who won't be in the Rose Garden that day? All the people who have been priced out of the market.

Politicians want to pass feel-good legislation. They will not put a human face to the costs they impose in order to do it.

## The Reality of the Minimum Wage for Workers

We talk about the minimum wage as if it were a restriction—a coercion—on employers. It is. But, odd as this might sound, the minimum wage is equally a restriction on workers.

The law prohibits people from working unless those people can find employers willing to pay them the minimum wage. The Mathews brothers had no work experience and little education. Their labor wasn't worth the minimum wage. But Brian Choi was willing to give them a chance to build some job skills by doing odd jobs for less than the minimum wage. To Choi, the

Mathewses' labor wasn't worth the minimum wage, but it was worth something. While the young men would have preferred to make a higher wage (who wouldn't?), they were willing to give up their time for less. But the minimum wage law prohibited them from selling their labor, because they could not obtain the mandated minimum.

And here we see an important truth about workers: a worker is really a small business that sells labor to customers whom we call "employers."

It is a common lament among unskilled workers that you can't get a job without experience, and you can't get experience without a job. The minimum wage is often the reason. When Choi was forced to pay the minimum wage, he had to let the Mathews brothers go. Without jobs, they lost access to valuable training and experience that would have helped them get jobs in the future.

All else being equal, people would rather be paid more. But if the choice is between a lower wage and no wage at all, many might prefer the lower wage. This is precisely what illegal workers across the country tell us every time they accept an under-the-table job at a below-minimum-wage rate.

The moral of the story is that the minimum wage is a double-edged sword. Does it help some low-wage workers? Absolutely. Does it help all low-wage workers? Absolutely not. And the harm it does to those it does harm is far greater than the help it provides to those it helps. When the minimum wage goes from $9 to $10, the full-time worker who manages to keep his job ends up $2,000 per year better off. But the full-time worker who is laid off ends up $18,000 per year worse off. And on average, the worker who is laid off is the lower-skilled worker—the one who will have the harder time finding another job.

It's not only workers on the fringes who might prefer to sell their labor for less than the minimum wage. There are always people working for much less than the minimum wage, or for no wage at all. Interns and apprentices offer their labor at a rock-bottom price, or even for free, in exchange for the opportunity to get experience and on-the-job training. These aren't careers. Like minimum wage jobs, internships and apprenticeships are stepping-stones to better positions.

But even these arrangements are now subject to government coercion. In 2010 the federal government adopted new rules limiting the conditions under which a for-profit employer can hire unpaid interns. The rules say that the employer may not be the "primary beneficiary" of the employment relationship.[6] Since the intern receives no pay, under the rules the value of the experience the intern gets from the internship must exceed whatever value the intern generates for the employer.

Interestingly, Congress has no such rule for its own interns. Why not? Because an internship on Capitol Hill "provides invaluable résumé-building experience," in the words of one Senator.[7] Apparently, politicians perceive that this might not be the case for interns in the for-profit world. The restrictions on unpaid internships remove one way in which potential workers and employers can cooperate, thereby making both worse off.

It is worth repeating: the people whom minimum wage legislation harms the most are the most vulnerable in the labor market in the first place. Proponents of the minimum wage present it as resolving a conflict between employers and low-wage employees. The reality is that the minimum wage creates a conflict between some low-wage employees and other low-wage employees.

## Myths About Minimum Wage Workers

Myths and misperceptions cloud the public's understanding of the minimum wage. One misconception is that minimum wage workers are some sort of static group. Much discussion seems to presuppose that the people earning minimum wage today are doomed to earn the minimum wage for the rest of their lives. The reality is that most minimum wage workers earn the minimum wage for a short while and then improve their situations. Who tells us this? The same federal government that gives us the minimum wage in the first place.

The Bureau of Labor Statistics tells us that most workers move out of minimum wage jobs quickly and are very unlikely to return to them. Of workers who start out at the minimum wage, 46 percent move on to earn more than the minimum within one year. Of workers still earning the minimum wage in their second year of work, 55 percent graduate to higher wages by their third year.[8] For every hundred workers who start their careers at the minimum wage, only three are still earning the minimum wage five years later. And this accounts for the few workers who slip back into the minimum wage after earning more.

Out of 147 million hourly and salaried workers in the United States in 2017, only 1.8 million earned at or below the federal

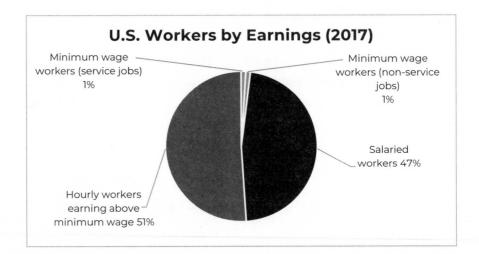

**U.S. Workers by Earnings (2017)**

Minimum wage workers (service jobs) 1%

Minimum wage workers (non-service jobs) 1%

Salaried workers 47%

Hourly workers earning above minimum wage 51%

*Data source: Bureau of Labor Statistics*

minimum wage.[9] That's just over 1 percent of all U.S. workers. Of the 1.8 million who worked at or below the federal minimum wage, 1.2 million also earned tips. Since tipped workers tend to earn significantly more than the minimum after tips, the number of workers actually earning the federal minimum wage was probably closer to 550,000.[10] This means that around one-third of 1 percent of U.S. workers earned the federal minimum wage that year.

This is not the public perception. Politicians and pundits make it seem as if vast numbers of Americans work for the minimum wage. Certainly, 550,000 is a lot of people, but relative to the total number of American workers, it is small.

Another misconception is that there are many older minimum wage workers. More than 60 percent of minimum wage workers are under the age of thirty. This means that about eight-tenths of one percent of American workers are over thirty and earning the minimum wage.[11]

Where do minimum wage workers work? Almost two-thirds of them work in service occupations. And almost three-quarters of those are specifically in food-preparation and food-serving

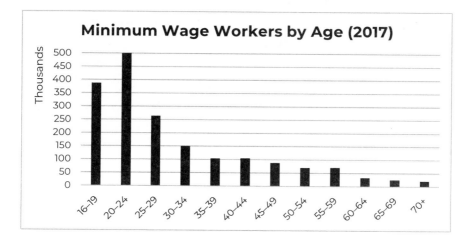

*Data source: Bureau of Labor Statistics*

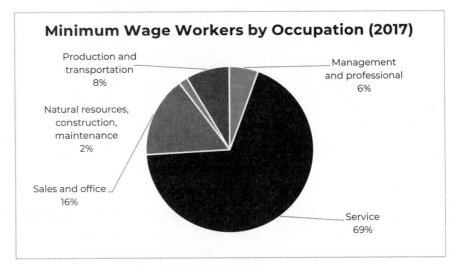

## Minimum Wage Workers by Occupation (2017)

Production and transportation 8%

Natural resources, construction, maintenance 2%

Sales and office 16%

Management and professional 6%

Service 69%

*Data source: Bureau of Labor Statistics*

jobs.[12] This may contribute to people's misconception that minimum wage workers are more numerous than they really are, as the average person encounters food service workers more often than workers in other industries.

The popular image of the full-time minimum wage worker is also false. Almost two-thirds of minimum wage workers work part time. Only 2 percent work more than forty hours per week.[13]

What does this mean? When politicians talk about raising the minimum wage, they talk about the single mother who is holding down two jobs to support her family. The reality is that the average minimum wage earner works part time and lives in a household with a family income of more than $53,000, which is about the median household income in the United States.[14]

## Why the Minimum Wage Is Unnecessary

Politicians often call for minimum wage protection by suggesting that wage regulation is the only thing stopping businesses

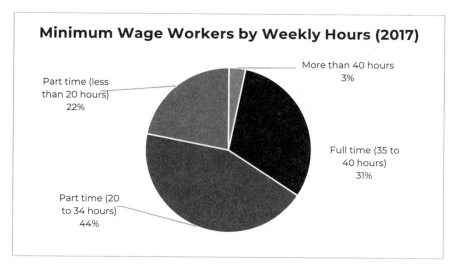

## Minimum Wage Workers by Weekly Hours (2017)

More than 40 hours
3%

Part time (less than 20 hours)
22%

Full time (35 to 40 hours)
31%

Part time (20 to 34 hours)
44%

*Data source: Bureau of Labor Statistics*

from paying almost nothing. But there is no law requiring employers to pay *more* than the minimum wage. If it is true that the minimum wage is what prevents employers from paying workers mere pennies an hour, then why don't all employers pay *exactly* the minimum wage? In fact, in 2019 nearly 99 percent of all U.S. workers earned more than the federal minimum of $7.25 per hour. Fully half of all full-time U.S. workers earned more than $21 per hour.[15]

Obviously, some other force—much stronger than minimum wage legislation—must prevent employers from paying their workers low wages. That force is competition.

Employers must compete with one another for labor. They compete by offering better working conditions, more flexible hours, better benefits—and higher wages. That nearly 99 percent of workers earn more than the federal minimum suggests that a better way to ensure workers receive higher wages is not to impose laws restricting wages but to remove laws restricting competition for workers. Other things being equal, the more competition there is among employers, the higher workers' wages will be.

Politicians claim that the minimum wage helps the least skilled and most vulnerable workers. But this is the group that is most likely to lose their jobs when the government tries to regulate hourly wages. The reason for this goes back to the ingredients that comprise the wage rate: the value of the completed work and the number of people capable of performing the work. On average, more skilled, educated, and experienced workers produce more value. A more productive worker can compete with a less productive worker for a job either because of the worker's greater productivity or by accepting a lower wage. But a less productive worker can compete with a more productive worker only by accepting a lower wage. By forcing up the price of workers, the minimum wage takes away the only competitive advantage less productive workers have.

We might not like to say it, but some people simply make better workers than others—whether because of education or experience or skills or personality or some other reason. These workers benefit from minimum wage increases. Less educated, less experienced, and less skilled workers lose almost every time.

When the price of something rises, people buy less of it. For an employer, labor is an expense just like any other. So when the government raises the minimum wage, employers hire fewer workers, or employ them for fewer hours, or both.

But that's not the only effect. As you might expect, when there is more money to be made from selling labor, more people look to sell their labor. When the government raises the minimum wage, people who previously weren't interested in working enter the labor market. Retirees, stay-at-home parents, the teenage children of more affluent families, and others join the labor pool. On average, these people tend to be higher-quality workers. Retirees tend to come with rich job experiences. Stay-at-home parents tend to be more diligent and to have previous work experience. Teenage children of affluent parents tend to be better educated. This flood of higher-quality minimum wage workers pushes the lower-quality minimum wage workers out of their jobs even more. The minimum wage has the effect, once again, of marginalizing the very people it was intended to protect.

Some minimum wage advocates argue that raising the minimum wage can increase worker productivity and so actually be good for businesses. Greater productivity isn't necessarily good for employers. It's good only if the value of the increased productivity exceeds the cost of obtaining the increased productivity. If it were true that a higher wage increased worker productivity, and that the increased productivity was worth more to the employer than the increased wage, then employers would voluntarily increase wages. If employers have to be coerced into raising wages, then we know that whatever increase in productivity might emerge is not worth the increased wage.

Average worker productivity does tend to increase as the minimum wage rises, but not for reasons that proponents of the minimum wage would have you believe. Instead, raising the minimum wage gives employers more of an incentive to lay off less productive workers. Average productivity then increases. Think of it this way: Following the outbreak of a virulent childhood disease, the average age of a population rises. But the childhood disease does not cause people to live longer. It increases the population's average age by killing off children.

Consider how the minimum wage affects workers with different educations.[16] Over the past thirty years, as the federal minimum wage has risen (relative to the average wage rate), unemployment among college-educated workers has not changed—but the unemployment rate among workers with only high school diplomas has risen, and the unemployment rate among workers with less than a high school education has risen even more.[17]

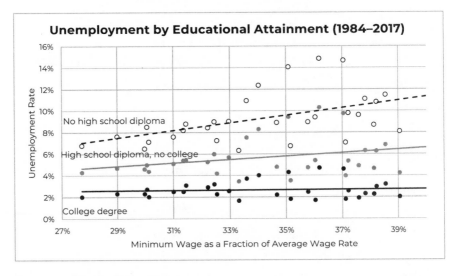

*Data source: Bureau of Labor Statistics*

Politicians *are* picking winners and losers, but they are lying about whom they've picked.

Finally, the money to pay for an increased minimum wage must come from somewhere. And it can come from only four places: other minimum wage workers, in the form of layoffs and reduced hours; higher wage workers, in the form of static or reduced compensation; investors, in the form of lower profits; or customers, in the form of higher prices. How much each group pays for the minimum wage hike depends on how competitive the various markets are.

When businesses face a lot of competition for investment funds, they will be less likely to pass on added costs to investors. When businesses face a lot of competition for customers, they will be less inclined to pass on the added costs to customers. When businesses face a lot of competition for high-skilled workers, they will be less inclined to pass on the added costs to those workers. Of all the markets in question, businesses tend to face the least competition in the market for low-skilled workers, which means those workers typically pay the lion's share of the cost of a minimum wage hike—usually in the form of unemployment.

As if all this weren't enough, employers also lower their labor costs with technology. When the cost of labor gets too high, it becomes cost-effective for employers to replace workers with machines. There was a time, barely remembered at this point (except in Oregon and New Jersey), when gas stations hired workers to pump customers' gas. Fast food workers once poured drinks. Grocery stores once had employees at every checkout lane. There were no self-service kiosks at fast food restaurants. Nearly every town in America had a video store. Some of these transitions, like the disappearance of video stores, have been due mostly to new and cheaper technologies. Some of the transitions, like asking fast food customers to fill their own cups, have been due largely to the increased cost of labor. The minimum wage has contributed to the disappearance of all these jobs.

What else happens when the government forces employers to pay more for labor? Two things: outsourcing and undocumented work. These are two ways, one legal and one not, that employers and potential employees try to get around the minimum wage barrier.

Outsourcing is simply the exporting of jobs. According to the Communications Workers of America, for example, U.S. firms outsourced 500,000 call-center jobs from 2006 to 2011.[18] Call-center jobs are not no-skill jobs, but they typically don't require higher education or special training. Because the work is done by telephone or online, these jobs are extremely easy to outsource. Consequently, as the minimum wage in the United States rises, employers have a greater incentive to send call-center jobs to countries where there is no minimum wage.

Undocumented labor is another effect. A rising minimum wage shuts low-skilled American workers out of the legal labor market. Employers have a greater incentive, where possible, to hire workers under the table. And these workers are not afforded any of the legal or financial protections extended to documented workers.

## Why Do We Have the Minimum Wage?

The minimum wage doesn't help the least advantaged workers. In fact, it makes their situation worse, increasing unemployment among the people least able to deal with it. So why do we have the minimum wage at all?

> **The minimum wage doesn't help the least advantaged workers—it makes their situation worse**

One answer is that many people who earn far more than the minimum benefit from it nonetheless. Politicians, for example.

Politicians seem to miss the negative consequences of the minimum wage every time they look to raise the rate. Or maybe they don't miss these things at all, because what they are really doing is buying votes. It may be more important to them to appear to be concerned with the working poor than to enact policies that will actually help the poor. And it is far easier to say, "Vote for me and I'll put more money in your pocket by raising the minimum wage" than it is to explain why the minimum wage is a bad idea. Because of this, politicians who lie about the minimum wage (or who simply care more about feelings than facts) will tend to win elections over opponents who know better and tell the truth about it.

This brings us not to the dirty little secret of the minimum wage but to the dirty *big* secret. Unions are one of the largest beneficiaries of minimum wage hikes, because many union wages are tied to the minimum wage.[19] When the minimum wage increases, many union contracts call for members' wages to rise automatically or for the reopening of wage negotiations. So when the minimum wage rises, union wages also tend to go up. And because union laborers tend to be more skilled, raising the minimum wage shuts out competition from less skilled and cheaper labor.

Maybe it isn't all that confusing, then, why so many politicians turn a blind eye to the actual effect of the minimum wage on marginal workers. The politicians who advocate hardest for the minimum wage are the very same politicians who support labor union activity most fervently. Who, after all, is the preferred constituency? Marginalized workers, or labor unions with deep pockets? The evidence is clear.[20] Political campaign donations from labor unions and individuals affiliated with unions peaked in 2016 at $217 million.[21] Almost 90 percent of these donations went to Democrats—the party that most strongly supports minimum wage hikes.

In the end, wages rise either because of market pressures or by government fiat—and these are simply different words for cooperation and coercion. Market wages emerge when workers are willing to accept what employers are willing to offer. Such wages are the result of cooperation. But when the government prohibits workers and employers from cooperating, it pushes the most vulnerable workers out of the labor market entirely. This will be good for some workers but harmful for others. This is the cost of setting wages by coercion rather than cooperation.

# 5

# GUN CONTROL

The gun control debate in America has a long and storied past, and it is not a single, continuous story. It is a sequence of stories about coercion, from the ratification of the Second Amendment in 1791 to our current hodgepodge of local, state, and federal laws regarding the ownership and use of firearms.

The first steps toward gun control in the United States were doubtlessly rooted in racism. The first gun control measures in this country, enacted after the Civil War, were designed to keep firearms out of the hands of newly freed slaves.[1]

These laws were part of the so-called Black Codes, which southern states passed in 1865 and 1866. The Black Codes regulated the lives of black people generally, and freed slaves specifically, after the Thirteenth Amendment eliminated slavery in the United States. The laws denied black people the right to own property, the right to move through public spaces, and the right to conduct business. Anti-vagrancy laws made it possible to prosecute black people for nearly every behavior of which white majorities disapproved.

Curtailing the freedoms of ex-slaves would be more difficult were those ex-slaves permitted to exercise their Second Amendment right of keeping and bearing arms. So the Black Codes denied black people that right. The first gun control legislation in the United States thus emerged as part of a larger attempt to keep former slaves in the South "down on the farm."

This was the extent of gun control for more than sixty years. Then Congress passed laws banning the mailing of concealable weapons (1927), regulating fully automatic weapons (1934), and placing limitations on who could legally sell, and in some instances purchase, firearms (1938).

It wasn't until the assassination of John F. Kennedy in 1963 that gun control went mainstream. The Gun Control Act of 1968 limited firearm possession according to age, criminal history, and mental competence. The federal government established an independent Bureau of Alcohol, Tobacco, and Firearms in 1972, in part to control the use and sale of firearms and to enforce federal gun laws.[2]

But the event that gave rise to our current gun control laws occurred in 1981, when John Hinckley Jr. attempted to assassinate President Ronald Reagan. On March 30, 1981, Hinckley fired six times at Reagan. One bullet struck the President in the chest, lodging just centimeters from his heart. White House Press Secretary James Brady suffered an even more serious injury: a bullet to his head caused brain damage and severe disabilities.

In the wake of the shooting, Brady's wife, Sarah, worked tirelessly on gun control. Her efforts helped produce the Brady Bill, which President Bill Clinton signed into law in 1993. The law provided for more stringent background checks on those who would purchase firearms and restricted who could legally ship or transport firearms.

More important, the rhetoric of gun control changed in the years after James Brady was so grievously injured. The rallying cry of "If it saves just one life…" came to echo through the gun control movement. It resonated with the public.

For example, in January 2013, President Barack Obama said, "If there's even one thing we can do to reduce this [gun] violence, if there's even one life that can be saved, then we've got an obligation to try." A month later he tweeted, "If we save even one life from gun violence, it's worth it." His Vice President, Joe Biden, backed up Obama, saying, "As the President said, if your actions result in only saving one life, they're worth taking."[3]

> **An argument intended to manipulate can stand on emotion. But an argument intended to persuade must stand on fact and reason.**

Politicians use such lines because they stir emotions. An argument intended to manipulate can stand on emotion. But an argument intended to persuade must stand on fact and reason. And politicians typically argue from emotion when facts and reason don't cooperate.

## If It Saves Just One Life…

When we turn our attention from deaths by guns to deaths by other causes, the emptiness of the "if it saves just one life" argument becomes very clear very quickly. Consider the "senseless violence" that occurs on American roads every year. We should do whatever we can if it saves just one life, no?

Let's see.

In late July 2012, a pickup truck packed with twenty-three people veered off a Texas highway and crashed into two trees.[4]

Nine people were injured in the crash, but they were the lucky ones. The other fourteen occupants of the truck were killed. In the aftermath, bodies lay everywhere. Among the dead were two children. Alcohol was not involved, and there was no evidence of another vehicle at the scene. The weather at the time of the crash was dry and clear.

So why was the call for legislation not swift and immediate after such a terrible event? Because people knew that these sorts of things happen from time to time, and there is little, if anything, that legislation can do to change that.

But that's not exactly true, is it? We could address automotive deaths at any time if we were truly committed to doing so. One piece of legislation could virtually guarantee that no one would ever die on American roads again. All we would have to do is to reduce the speed limit on every road in the country to five miles per hour. That would save more than just one life.

Of course, everyone knows that imposing a national speed limit of five miles per hour is ludicrous. It also would do more harm than good. Think about it. The cost of policing would rise dramatically because almost everyone would want to drive much faster than five miles per hour. This would leave fewer police resources available for preventing and investigating other crimes. Few people would have the time to commute more than five miles or so, and even a commute that short would take two hours every day. But the law would do more than upend lives. We might all starve because we would have profound difficulties keeping grocery stores stocked with food. We would also have trouble getting people to lifesaving medical care quickly. Many people would, in fact, die because we passed a law intended to save lives.

And yet the "if it saves just one life" argument comes out every time gun violence captures the national attention. We should ban "assault weapons" if it saves just one life. We should heighten firearm licensure requirements if it saves just one life.

We should limit the number of bullets a magazine can hold if it saves just one life.

The "if it saves just one life" argument is usually nonsense. All human actions involve trade-offs. As the speed-limit example illustrates, a gain in one direction inevitably leads to losses in another. There is probably no such thing as a law that universally saves lives. There are only laws that save lives in one place in exchange for losing lives in another.

Consider gun violence in Texas. Most people are aware that Texas currently has some of the most lenient gun laws in the nation, but this was not always the case. In 1991 it was illegal to carry a firearm in a public place, so when Suzanna Hupp went to lunch with her parents at Luby's Cafeteria in Killeen in October of that year, she left her handgun in her locked car to comply with the law.[5] She was, after all, a good, law-abiding citizen. And this would come to haunt her for the rest of her life.

George Hennard, sadly, was not inclined to comply with the law. He crashed his pickup truck through the front window of the restaurant, got out, and began shooting at everyone inside. Hupp reported reaching for her purse to retrieve her pistol, only then remembering that it was locked in her car a hundred feet away. Between her and her weapon, Hennard was busy shooting fifty people, killing twenty-three in the process. Hupp's father, Al Gratia, rushed Hennard in an ill-fated attempt to stop the massacre. Hennard shot him in the chest, and Gratia died just feet away from his wife and daughter. At this point Hupp ran, ultimately escaping through an open window. She assumed her mother was right behind her but later learned that her mother instead ran to her husband's side, where Hennard shot her in the head. Several police were attending a conference at the hotel next door. But since the hotel manager had asked them not to carry their weapons into the hotel so as not to offend the guests, they lost precious time going to their cars to retrieve their guns.

There can be no doubt that the intent of the state of Texas in limiting its citizens' ability to carry concealed weapons in public was to limit gun violence within its borders. The unintended consequence, however, was to disarm law-abiding citizens like Suzanna Hupp. George Hennard, already planning on ignoring the prohibition against murder, was not going to be dissuaded by the same law that had Hupp lock her weapon in her car. By following the law, Hupp left herself exposed to the random violence that resulted in the deaths of her parents and twenty-one other human beings. However many lives Texas's gun law might have saved, twenty-three deaths could have been prevented had it not been for that same law.

As you can see, no law on either side of the issue would have saved "just one life." There were only trade-offs to be considered. Disarming the citizenry might well save some lives. Crimes of passion and crimes of opportunity are undoubtedly mitigated when no one has immediate access to firearms in the heat of the moment, for example. But the same act of disarming law-abiding people left everyone at Luby's on October 16, 1991, at the mercy of a single man bent on killing.

When politicians say, "If it saves just one life," they can appear to care deeply while simultaneously absolving themselves of the responsibility of crafting a rational response to a difficult issue. It allows them to trade on emotions instead of facts.

If we really believed that any law is justified if it saves just one life, we would require all Americans to pass a mental health evaluation on a regular basis or be institutionalized (more than 38,000 Americans commit suicide annually). We would outlaw all motor vehicles (almost 35,000 Americans die in vehicle accidents annually). We would require all houses to be single-story structures (more than 26,000 die in falls annually). We would ban alcohol (almost 17,000 die annually from alcohol-related liver disease). We would require people to be certified as swimmers before allowing them into any large body of water (more than 3,500 die from drowning annually). We would prohibit women from getting pregnant unless they had no family history of birth complications (more than 900 American women die in childbirth annually).[6]

Of course, none of these things will ever happen, nor should they. Life is full of dangers that cannot be legislated away.

## What About the Trade-Offs?

Reasonable people understand that there are valuable trade-offs when it comes to cars, food, alcohol, and numerous other things that we keep using despite the cost in lives.

But many reasonable people say that trade-offs simply don't apply in the case of guns. In fact, the question of trade-offs lies at the core of the disagreement in the gun control debate. Gun control advocates don't see any trade-off in banning guns, because they don't see any benefit to owning a gun. Meanwhile, gun-rights advocates see a significant trade-off, because they see the safety benefits of carrying guns.

What makes it easy to dismiss the possibility of trade-offs are the horrific anecdotes of gun violence. Twenty children and six adults died at the shooting at Sandy Hook Elementary School on December 14, 2012.[7] Thirty-two students and faculty members died and another seventeen were wounded at the Virginia Tech shooting in April 2007. Five died and twenty-one were wounded at the Northern Illinois University shooting in February 2008. Following these tragedies came shootings at Umpqua Community College in 2015 and Marshall County High School, Marjory Stoneman Douglas High School, and Santa Fe High School, all in 2018.

In the Sandy Hook massacre, most victims were just six or

seven years old. It was, quite understandably, more than the American people could take. The political reaction was swift, and it extended all the way to the President of the United States. President Obama almost immediately called on Congress to pass gun control legislation.

The legislation languished and eventually died in Congress, but the President pushed forward with his own agenda. He issued twenty-three executive orders to address what he termed "the broader epidemic of gun violence in this country."[8] He also ordered the Centers for Disease Control and Prevention (CDC) to research the causes and prevention of gun violence. The National Academies' Institute of Medicine and National Research Council, to which the CDC assigned the research problem, completed the project in a matter of months.

And that's where the story of gun violence took a turn.

The study concluded that there was no "epidemic of gun violence" in the United States.[9] The majority of firearms deaths in the United States from 2000 to 2010—61 percent of them—were suicides. Comparatively, the types of mass shootings that gave rise to the study in the first place were exceedingly rare.

Since 2010, however, the data look different. *Mother Jones* reported that the number of mass shootings (shootings with at least three victims) averaged 1.8 per year from 1982 through 2010.[10] But from 2011 through 2018, the average jumped to 7—an almost fourfold increase. The average number of victims per incident also jumped from 28 from 1982 through 2010 to 172 from 2011 through 2018.

These numbers appear alarming. And every life lost should be a cause for concern. But perspective is important when people are calling for the government to establish and enforce policies intended to address a problem—policies that will have unintended consequences, including some that run counter to the policies' goals. The 167 people killed in U.S. mass shootings in

2018 represented five-ten-thousandths of 1 percent of all people who died in the United States that year, and eight-tenths of 1 percent of all people murdered in the United States that year.[11] With respect not only to deaths in general but also to murders specifically, mass shootings are extremely rare.

You would never know this by watching television. Although mass shootings account for a fraction of a fraction of murders, media coverage of them has skyrocketed. Why? Because the media sells advertising, not news. And violence sells. We don't have an epidemic of mass shootings; we have an epidemic of opportunism. How do you know? Because statistics on gun violence tend to get less attention than do anecdotes about gun violence.

To put mass shootings in perspective, 1,600 times the number of Americans are killed annually on roads as in mass shootings. Of course, one is often the result of human error or inattention, while the other is almost always the result of a deranged mind. But in the end, a life lost is just that: a life lost.

Further, the number of gun-related suicides dwarfs the number of gun-related mass killings. There were almost 300,000 gun-related suicides from 2000 through 2015, for an average of more than 18,500 per year.[12] This is a problem, but it is surely not the problem that people are talking about when they refer to the "epidemic of gun violence." We react to sensationalistic media coverage of the events that claim the fewest lives, diverting our attention from those that claim the most.

The National Research Council's report also stated, "Almost all national survey estimates indicate that defensive gun uses by victims are at least as common as offensive uses by criminals."[13] Perhaps more striking than this, those who defend themselves with firearms are considerably less likely to be injured or killed than those who do not.

It turns out that there is a trade-off to banning guns. So

banning guns can't be about "saving just one life" any more than banning cars or alcohol or high-cholesterol foods can.

Had Suzanna Hupp carried her gun with her, she might have been able to stop George Hennard after only one person had died. Even if the police—who were right next door—had had their guns at the ready and come immediately, more than one person would have been dead by the time they arrived. All the Texas gun law did was to ensure that Hennard was the only person in Luby's armed that day.

Or consider the case of Melinda Herman. On January 4, 2013, she and her two young children were in their Georgia home when they heard an intruder break in.[14] Mrs. Herman and her children fled to the attic, locking doors behind them. They listened as the intruder, Paul Slater, broke down the doors with a crowbar and approached the attic. When Slater opened the attic door, Mrs. Herman shot him. Slater survived, but the shots brought him down, allowing the Hermans to escape.

Had Melinda Herman not been armed, she and her children would have ended up as casualties, and Slater would have been gone long before the police arrived.

It is true that an armed criminal is more powerful than an unarmed criminal. But an armed criminal and an armed victim are equally powerful, regardless of differences in height, weight, build, and gender. Conversely, an unarmed criminal can be much more powerful than an unarmed victim, particularly when the unarmed victim is a woman, elderly, or physically slight. Seen in this light, guns eliminate power inequality.

## What's Responsible for Gun Violence?

According to Gallup polls, the percentage of U.S. households that reported having a gun in the home has fluctuated between

34 percent and 51 percent from 1959 through the present. The
overall trend since 1959 has moved down slightly but not significantly.[15] The question people tend to ask is, what has happened to gun-related homicides over time as gun ownership has
changed? But the gun-homicide rate isn't really what's important. Ultimately, we don't care *how* people are murdered. We
care *that* people are murdered. Someone intent on murder can
use a fist, a knife, or many other objects. So it is important to
look at the homicide rate rather than the gun-homicide rate—
especially if there is any truth to the claim that the defensive use
of guns can reduce homicides.

According to FBI data, the homicide rate has fluctuated
between 4.5 and 10.1 per 100,000 people since 1960.[16] Over
the decades, the homicide and gun-ownership rates sometimes
moved together, sometimes moved in opposite directions; sometimes one moved while the other didn't. Statistically, there is no
significant relationship between the two rates.[17]

But regular homicides, while deplorable, typically aren't
what spur citizens to action. What gets us mad enough to want

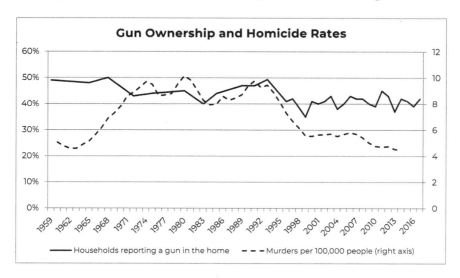

Data sources: Gallup and Bureau of Justice Statistics

to do something are mass shootings. People simply assume that mass shootings are on the rise because of the proliferation of guns. If there were fewer guns, they conclude, we'd have fewer mass shootings.

But there is no apparent relationship between the mass-shooting fatality rate and the gun-ownership rate.[18]

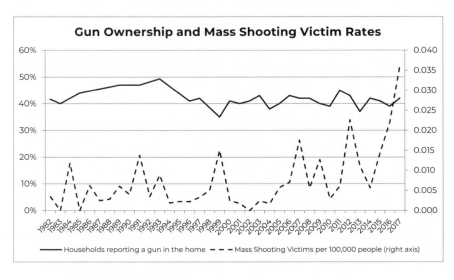

*Data sources: Gallup and* Mother Jones

There are two beneficial effects to having fewer guns. One is a lower suicide rate. If we arrange the states in order from those with the highest reported rates of gun ownership (led by Alaska, Wyoming, and Montana) to those with the lowest (led by Hawaii, New Jersey, and Massachusetts) and then compare suicide rates across the states, a pattern emerges. States with higher reported gun-ownership rates also have higher suicide rates (on average) than do states with lower reported gun-ownership rates. For example, Alaska has a much higher gun-ownership rate (60 percent) than does Massachusetts (10 percent), and Alaska's suicide rate is almost eight times that of

Massachusetts. New Hampshire and Vermont have nearly identical climates and incomes, yet Vermont's gun-ownership rate
and suicide rate are both 1.4 times those of New Hampshire.
There are exceptions, but on average, states in which people have
greater access to guns also have higher suicide rates.[19]

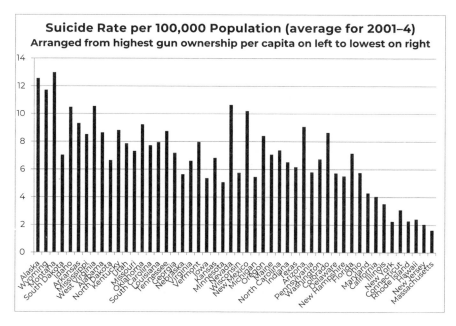

**Suicide Rate per 100,000 Population (average for 2001–4)**
Arranged from highest gun ownership per capita on left to lowest on right

*Data source: Centers for Disease Control and Prevention*

Another benefit to fewer guns is fewer accidental shooting
deaths. The fewer guns there are, the fewer opportunities people
have to shoot someone accidentally or to get shot. And the data
bear this out. States with higher reported rates of gun ownership
also (on average) have higher rates of accidental shootings.[20]

The number of accidental shooting deaths, however, is
extremely small compared to firearm suicide and homicide
deaths. From 1999 through 2011, fewer than 700 people died
per year from accidental shootings versus almost 18,000 per year
from suicides and 12,000 per year from intentional shootings.[21]

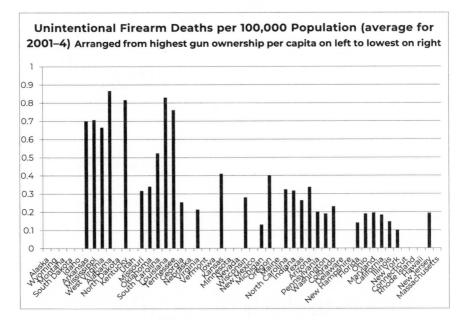

**Unintentional Firearm Deaths per 100,000 Population (average for 2001–4)** Arranged from highest gun ownership per capita on left to lowest on right

*Data source: Centers for Disease Control and Prevention*

Every death should be cause for concern. But deaths from accidents and suicides can be better addressed through more focused means than banning guns. Accidents are a safety issue that can be addressed through training and technology, like gun locks and smart guns. Banning guns isn't necessary. Suicide stems from mental conditions that require treatment. Trying to treat suicide by banning guns is like trying to treat alcoholism by banning six-packs.

The deaths that are the main drivers behind the push to ban guns are intentional shootings. Yet here, something odd emerges in the data.[22] Unlike what we see with suicides and accidental shootings, there is no clear relationship between gun ownership and intentional shootings.

If it were true that restricting people's access to guns reduced the firearm homicide rate, then we should observe lower firearm homicide rates in states with lower gun-ownership rates

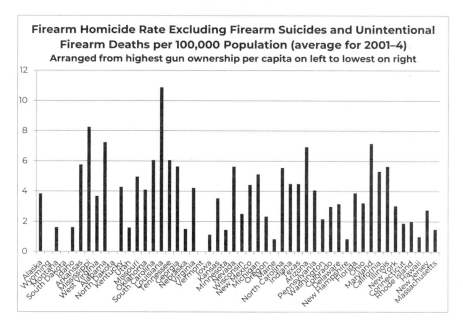

**Firearm Homicide Rate Excluding Firearm Suicides and Unintentional Firearm Deaths per 100,000 Population (average for 2001–4)**
Arranged from highest gun ownership per capita on left to lowest on right

*Data source: Centers for Disease Control and Prevention*

and higher firearm homicide rates among states with higher gun-ownership rates—just as we saw for suicides and accidental shootings. Yet no such pattern emerges.

There simply is no pattern. Yes, Alaska offers people much greater access to guns than does Massachusetts, and Alaska's firearm homicide rate is 2.6 times that of Massachusetts. But Massachusetts and Nebraska have the same gun-homicide rates, while Nebraska's gun-ownership rate is four times that of Massachusetts. Meanwhile, Mississippi has the same gun-ownership rate as Utah and Idaho, yet Mississippi's gun-homicide rate is almost five times that of the other two states. Montana's gun-ownership rate is more than double Maryland's, yet Maryland's gun-homicide rate is more than four times Montana's.

The absence of a pattern also appears among cities. It is legal to carry a gun in Pittsburgh but not in Philadelphia, yet Pittsburgh's gun-homicide rate is 37 percent lower than Philadelphia's. It is

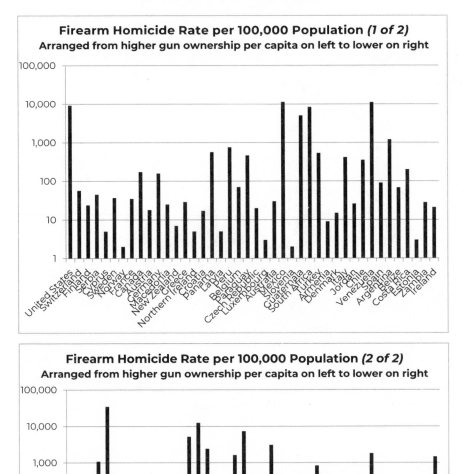

**Firearm Homicide Rate per 100,000 Population *(1 of 2)***
Arranged from higher gun ownership per capita on left to lower on right

**Firearm Homicide Rate per 100,000 Population *(2 of 2)***
Arranged from higher gun ownership per capita on left to lower on right

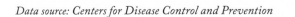

*Data source: Centers for Disease Control and Prevention*

legal to carry a gun in Atlanta but not in Chicago, but Atlanta's gun-homicide rate is 50 percent higher than Chicago's.[23]

No pattern exists among countries either. The United States has 11 times the number of guns per capita as does Brazil (88.8 per 100 people for the U.S. versus 8 per 100 people for Brazil), yet Brazil's gun-homicide rate is 4 times that of the United States. Switzerland and Finland have the same number of guns per capita (about 45 per 100 people for each country), yet Switzerland's gun-homicide rate is 2.4 times Finland's.[24]

Gun control proponents point to Australia's 1996 gun ban as evidence that gun control reduces firearm homicides. In Australia's case, an initial look at the data appears compelling. Gun homicides fell from an average of 71 per year in the seven years prior to the ban to 55 per year in the seven years after the ban. That's a 22 percent decline![25]

But a closer look reveals two concerning things. First, knife homicides in Australia appear to move in the opposite direction to gun homicides. Knife homicides outnumbered gun homicides by more than 2 to 1 prior to the gun ban, and more than 3 to 1 after. This suggests that, at least in a portion of the cases, the

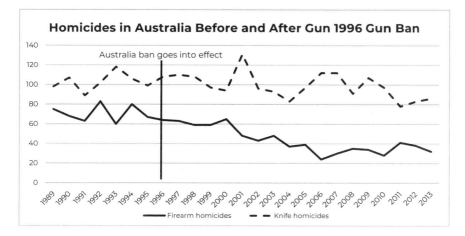

*Data source: Australian Institute of Criminology*

gun ban didn't reduce homicides but rather caused the perpetra-
tors to switch weapons. Australia's knife and gun homicides,
combined, fell only 8 percent in the seven-year period following the gun ban compared to the seven-year period preceding
the ban. This is a much less impressive story than the reported
22 percent decline in gun homicides.

Second, if we compare the same two seven-year periods in
the United States, we find that annual U.S. homicides fell from
an average of 23,267 to an average of 16,432. That's a 29 percent decline versus Australia's 22 percent decline. The United
States, without a gun ban, experienced a larger relative decline
in homicides than did Australia with the ban![26]

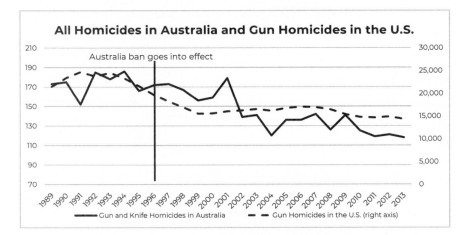

*Data sources: Australian Institute of Criminology and Centers for Disease Control and Prevention*

Finally, the homicide data leave out an extremely important point. To contribute to the homicide data, a gun must be
fired and kill someone. Guns can be fired without killing, and
they can be used to threaten without being fired. The Bureau of
Justice Statistics maintains records on instances in which crime
victims protect themselves with a gun, either by firing the gun
or *threatening* to fire the gun.[27] Over the five years from 2007

through 2011, there were 235,700 instances in which potential victims of violent crime defended themselves with a gun in the United States. Over the same period, there were 64,695 gun deaths (excluding suicides)—including deaths in which the potential victim killed the criminal.

In other words, from 2007 through 2011, potential victims used guns (either by firing or threatening to fire) in defense against violent crime well over three times as often as someone used a gun to kill another. And this ignores gun use in defense against property crime. From 2007 through 2011, potential victims either fired or threatened to fire guns in defense of property crime 103,000 times. In total, Americans used guns defensively more than five times as often as they used guns to murder people.[28]

There are some reasonable criticisms of these numbers. For example, they ignore instances in which the *criminal* didn't fire but threatened the victim with a gun. But they also ignore instances in which the victim might have used a gun had he been allowed to do so. For example, from 2007 through 2011, potential victims used weapons other than guns in defense against violent or property crime 429,300 times. Some of those potential victims used non-gun weapons only because gun laws made using a gun difficult (or in some states, nearly impossible).

The moral of the story goes back to trade-offs: Making it harder to obtain guns makes it harder for criminals to commit crimes. But making it harder to obtain guns also makes it harder for victims to defend themselves, thus making it easier for criminals to commit crimes.

Clearly, there are factors that influence, both positively and negatively, gun homicides. If our concern is reducing homicides, then we should focus first on identifying what those factors are. Every hour and every dollar we spend trying to reduce gun ownership is an hour and a dollar that we are not spending on the real causes of gun homicide. We might not be sure what those real causes are, but mental health is a strong contender. And to the extent that we are unsure what the real causes are, our time and dollars would be better spent finding out.

> **Making it harder to obtain guns makes it harder for crime victims to defend themselves**

What we can be sure of is that the gun debate is a boon for politicians on both sides of the aisle. Whether they are pro- or anti-gun, politicians get to use this emotionally charged issue in their bids for office. And they need never fear that the issue will go away, because data suggest that the solution they debate— restricting access to guns—will do little to limit homicides. In a perverse way, it's beneficial to politicians that they not resolve the gun problem in either direction. So long as the problem remains, politicians can continue to use it to attract votes.

The real lesson here is that even when we commit to using the powerful tool of coercion, even when we are convinced that its use is utterly warranted, we might not get anything resembling the results we intended. Coercion is not a magic wand; it is simply a tool. If it actually has no effect on the problem, as the data indicate here, the only effect coercion achieves is to limit people's freedom. Where gun violence is concerned, coercion is not the correct tool for the job, and emotive posturing will never change that.

# 6

# WARS ON NOUNS

The United States has fought twelve major wars since the Founding. Adjusted for inflation, the total cost of these twelve wars, not counting lives lost and property destroyed, reached almost $7 trillion.[1] In each of them, with the exception of the Vietnam War, the government clearly identified the enemy and specified a clear and achievable goal that would signal victory. By contrast, the war in Vietnam featured a somewhat nondescript enemy, shifting alliances, and goalposts that moved significantly as the conflict escalated.

In addition to those twelve wars, both declared like World War II and undeclared like the Korean conflict, the United States began fighting three others in the twentieth century and is still fighting them today. They have all been declared, in a way, but they ultimately share more in common with the Vietnam War than with any other. Enemies are ill defined, victory is indescribable (or indeed, impossible), strategies and tactics seem to change with the political winds, and resolve, on the part of both those who fight and those who endure, has been replaced with a form of tired resignation.

For all of these reasons, these wars—the wars on poverty, drugs, and terror—are unwinnable. And because they are unwinnable, they will also tend to be perpetual.

Times of war are the most coercive times self-governing regimes face, and politicians get to act with far freer hands when the rules of regular life are suspended during times of conflict. Throughout U.S. history, everything from conscription to product rationing to massive government spending flowed from the decision to make war. The price people paid in the form of dead, maimed, and injured loved ones is incalculable. But everyone knows going in that this sort of cost will be the inevitable outcome. Wars are expensive in every way imaginable.

Sometimes they are clearly worth the cost. World War II is the prime example. That war cost more than $4 trillion, adjusted for inflation.[2] More than 400,000 Americans died in the conflict, and more than 670,000 were wounded. In dollar terms, it was the most expensive military endeavor the United States ever undertook, but few would doubt its necessity. The forces of totalitarianism stood ready to overtake the globe, and their defeat in all likelihood averted a dark age for humanity.

Not all wars are so clear in their import, and when we add ill-defined or impossible standards of victory to the language of war, morasses ensue. This was the case with the Vietnam War, and it is the case with the various wars against nouns. The wars against poverty, drugs, and terror are all morasses of the worst kind: the kind that bring with them the coercion of wartime. The state brings its full coercive power to bear, not on foreign powers but on ourselves.

The only instance in which the Constitution explicitly permits the government to suspend people's rights wholesale appears in Article I, Section 9. The clause stipulates that the right not to be held without charge or trial (known as "habeas corpus") may be suspended in cases of "rebellion or invasion." During the Civil War, President Lincoln suspended the right of habeas corpus. During World War II, President Roosevelt took this a step further when he signed Executive Order 9066, which ordered all Americans of Japanese descent to report to internment camps.[3] During the Korean War, President Truman seized private steel mills to ensure uninterrupted steel production for the war effort. These Presidents met with differing responses from the Supreme Court, but in each case, the state of war emboldened them to exercise greater coercion.

> **The wars on poverty, drugs, and terror are unwinnable, and so they will be perpetual**

America's wars on nouns have also been vehicles for coercion.

## The War on Poverty

President Lyndon Johnson declared "all-out war on human poverty and unemployment in these United States" in his 1964 State of the Union address. The curious thing, though, is that the poverty rate in the United States was already declining prior to the declaration of this war. The U.S. poverty rate fell from 22.4 percent in 1959 to 19.5 percent in 1963. By the end of 1964, it stood at 19 percent.[4] The poverty rate then declined steadily from 1965 until 1973, when it bottomed out at 11.1 percent. After that, the poverty rate rose again. In the several decades since, it has averaged 13 percent, rising as high as 15.2 percent.[5] What we have been waging war on since about 1973 is unclear. If it is poverty, we have to admit that we are not winning.

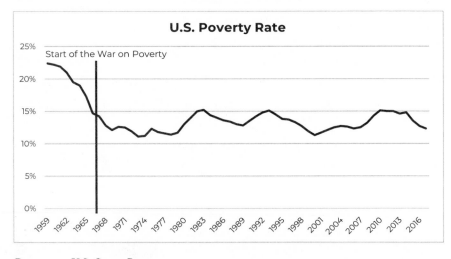

*Data source: U.S. Census Bureau*

In the first half century after President Johnson launched the war on poverty, the U.S. government spent more than $22 trillion (in inflation-adjusted dollars) on anti-poverty measures. That's more than three times what the United States has spent on all the actual wars it has fought in its history—combined. And the $22 trillion does not include Social Security and Medicare spending.[6]

This spending has bought a Byzantine set of programs that has included the Earned Income Tax Credit; the Refundable Child Credit; the Make Work Pay Tax Credit; Temporary Assistance for Needy Families (TANF, formerly Aid to Families with Dependent Children); Title IV-E Foster Care; Title IV-E Adoption Assistance; General Assistance; Refugee Assistance; General Assistance to Indians; Assets for Independence; State Children's Health Insurance Program (SCHIP); Medical General Assistance; Consolidated Health Center/Community Health Centers; Maternal and Child Health; Medical Assistance to Refugees; Healthy Start; Supplemental Nutrition Assistance Program (SNAP, formerly Food Stamps); School Lunch

Program; Special Supplemental Nutrition Program for Women, Infants, and Children (WIC); School Breakfast; Child Care Food Program; Nutrition Program for the Elderly; Commodity Supplemental Food Program; Temporary Emergency Food Program (TEFAP); Needy Families; Farmers' Market Nutrition Program; Special Milk Program; Section 8 Housing; Public Housing; Low-Income Housing Tax Credit for Developers; Home Investment Partnership Program; Homeless Assistance Grants; State Housing Expenditures; Rural Housing Insurance Fund; Rural Housing Service; Housing for the Elderly; Native American Housing with Disabilities; Low-Income Home Energy Assistance Program (LIHEAP); Universal Service Fund Subsidized Low-Income Phone Service; Pell Grants; Title I Grants to Local Education Authorities; Twenty-First Century Learning Centers; Special Programs for Disadvantaged Students; Supplemental Education Opportunity Grants; Adult Basic Education Grants; Migrant Education; Gear-Up; LEAP (formerly State Student Incentive Grant Program); Education for Homeless Children and Youth; Even Start; Aid for Graduate and Professional Study for Disadvantaged and Minorities; TANF Work Activities and Training; Job Corps; WIA Youth Opportunity Grants (formerly Summer Youth Employment); Senior Community Service Employment; WIA Adult Employment and Training (formerly JTPA IIA Training for Disadvantaged Adults and Youth); Food Stamp Employment and Training Program; Foster Grandparents; YouthBuild; Migrant Training; Native American Training; TANF Block Grant Services; Title XX Social Services Block Grant; Community Service Block Grant; Social Services for Refugees, Asylees, and Humanitarian Cases; Safe and Stable Families; Title III Aging Americans Act; Legal Services Block Grant; Family Planning; Emergency Food and Shelter Program; Healthy Marriage and Responsible Fatherhood Grants; Independent Living (Chafee Foster Care Independence

Program); Independent Living Training Vouchers; Maternal,
Infant, and Early Childhood Home Visiting Program; Head
Start; Childcare and Child Development Block Grant; Child-
care Entitlement to the States; TANF Block Grant Child Care;
Community Development Block Grant and Related Develop-
ment Funds; Economic Development Administration; Depart-
ment of Appalachian Regional Development; Empowerment
Zones; and Enterprise Communities Renewal.

So that's the war on poverty in a large, painful nutshell. And
for all that money, time, and effort, we have seen no significant
change in the United States poverty rate for more than forty-five
years. President Ronald Reagan had a clear idea of what had
happened when he remarked, in his 1988 State of the Union
address, "My friends, some years ago, the federal government
declared war on poverty, and poverty won."

So why do we persist?

There are a few answers. The most charitable among them
is that we are really trying to end poverty, but even if that goal
is ultimately unachievable, we are doing what we can to hold it
at bay.

A better, more explanatory answer is found between the lines
of the list above. We have developed both a poverty industry and
a poverty bureaucracy since 1964, and both of them seek to per-
petuate themselves. When has the head of any federal agency said
something like: "We have spent more than $22 trillion and yet
the poverty rate remains the same year over year. Clearly, none of
this is working, so we should stop wasting the money." Instead,
we hear something like: "We have not achieved our goal of elimi-
nating poverty, but just imagine how terrible things would have
been had we not spent $22 trillion on all of these programs."

We continue down the same unsuccessful path because, now
that it has been established, many people's livelihoods depend on
its continued existence. And those people have a strong incen-

tive to ensure that any meaningful "reforms" involve increased funding.

What gets lost is the original goal: ending poverty. We have come to accept poverty as a chronic condition requiring all manner of expensive treatment. But we never ask whether maybe we would have been better off not filtering all that money through the myriad programs and departments the government has created.

In fact, if the government had simply divided the $22 trillion among all the poor people living in the United States since 1964, each person would have received more than $10,000 per year. This would have reduced the poverty rate to nearly zero.

## The War on Drugs

President Richard Nixon declared a war on drugs in 1971, when he said:

> Public enemy No. 1 in the United States is drug abuse. In order to fight and defeat this enemy, it is necessary to wage a new, all-out offensive. I have asked the Congress to provide the legislative authority and the funds to fuel this kind of an offensive. This will be a worldwide offensive dealing with the problems of sources of supply...wherever they are in the world.[7]

The President asked for $84 million to begin the fight. Since then, the federal and state governments have spent more than $1 trillion fighting the war on drugs.[8] Let that sink in a moment. We have spent more than a trillion dollars fighting what amounts to a product that some people want to sell and other people want to purchase.

The war on drugs became law in 1972, borrowing significantly and purposefully from Lyndon Johnson's war on poverty language from not even a decade before. The federal government has been about as successful in its war on drugs as it has been in its war on poverty. The war on drugs has, at least, cost less over about the same span of years. But as is always the case with public policy, we should ask whether what we have obtained was worth the cost, and if the policy has yielded the sorts of behaviors we want.

What kinds of behaviors have we obtained? To begin, a good number of Americans have found themselves wrapped up in the expensive, time-consuming, and demoralizing American criminal justice system. Since the war on drugs began, around sixty million Americans have been arrested on drug charges. As a result of creating a victimless crime, the United States has become, in some ways (and especially in some places and directed toward some people), a police state. Since 2003, more than ten thousand police officers nationwide have been assigned full time to various drug task forces. This is, coincidentally, the size of a military division, and it is approximately the same number of soldiers that the United States had stationed in Afghanistan in 2017.

Take, for example, the county sheriff in Kansas who in 2012 saw a man and his children walk out of a hydroponic gardening store.[9] There is nothing illegal about hydroponic gardening stores, or anything they sell. In fact, the son needed the equipment to grow hydroponic tomatoes for a school project. Yet, because hydroponics *can be* used to grow marijuana, the police wrote down the man's license plate number, found his house, and then rifled through the family's trash when they left it out at the curb for removal. In the trash, the sheriff found "saturated plant material," otherwise known as wet leaves. The wet leaves led to a search warrant, which led to the police's holding the family at gunpoint for two hours as they ransacked the home looking for drugs.

The wet leaves, it turns out, were tea.

In 2014, police in Georgia raided a home at 2:15 in the morning.[10] Ten officers armed with military weapons and armor battered down the front door, threw in a flash-bang grenade, and stood back. When the police entered, they found that they had thrown the grenade into a playpen where a baby was sleeping. The baby suffered severe burns on his face and chest. The police found no drugs in the home and were not indicted for injuring the child.

These sorts of stories have become so common that they scarcely raise eyebrows when reported. People make mistakes, sometimes people die, sometimes people get civil settlements, and life goes on as before. But good public policy addresses an obvious problem, does so in the most cost-effective and least intrusive way possible, and is worth at least as much as it costs. What have we gotten for $1 trillion?

American drug policy classifies American citizens as enemy combatants—it is a war, after all. Worse, the drug war has stretched to the far corners of the globe. Our government routinely uses the U.S. military to stem the flow, into our country, of things that Americans want.

This is what happens when we declare war on a noun. The enemy becomes unclear, and when the enemy is unclear, sooner or later the enemy becomes everyone. The innocents who are traumatized, injured, or killed are simply collateral damage. To drug war proponents, people who are guilty of nothing that would harm anyone but themselves got what they had coming.

Perhaps most concerning, the Constitution itself has become a casualty of this war. Article I, Section 8, specifies the powers of Congress; nowhere does it say anything about "regulating drugs" or any similar authority. To the contrary, the drug war appears to violate the property rights protections that the Fourth Amendment defines quite directly.

But the constitutional damage goes far deeper than this.

We now live in an era in which we have to contend with civil asset forfeiture—a legal tool by which law enforcement can take a person's property without trial. If law enforcement has reason to believe that a person's property was acquired through criminal means, then they can and often do confiscate that property. To get the property back, the person must prove that the property was *not* acquired in an illegal endeavor. In effect, he is presumed guilty.

Not surprisingly, many instances of civil asset forfeiture arise from drug cases. The reasons for this are so clear that people in positions of authority seem to have absolutely no trouble admitting them. Consider that this appears in a Department of Justice publication:

> *The Need for Forfeiture*
>
> For many years, law enforcement agencies around the nation have faced shrinking budgets. Police administrators have been forced to develop creative budgeting strategies, such as securing federal grants and partnering with community foundations. Though it is an enforcement tool, asset forfeiture can assist in the budgeting realm by helping to offset the costs associated with fighting crime. Doing what it takes to undermine the illicit drug trade is expensive and time consuming. Forfeiture can help agencies target these difficult problems, sometimes without the need to seek additional outside resources to offset their costs.[11]

So law enforcement has an incentive to believe that all kinds of property are used in, or acquired as a result of, the commission of crimes. Today more Americans lose their property to police in the form of civil asset forfeiture than they do to criminals.[12]

The drug war has expanded steadily since President Nixon declared it in 1971, and as it has, both the rights and the bank accounts of American taxpayers and citizens have eroded. But how could it be any other way? We have declared war on something that people want and are willing to pay for. Three of the past four Presidents, men who prosecuted the drug war themselves, had at least at one point in their lives taken illegal drugs.

Given all of this, is it any wonder we have no chance of winning such a war? We cannot even define what winning the drug war would entail. This is not a recipe for good public policy; it is a recipe for perpetual coercion.

And as luck would have it, there is yet a third noun on which we have declared war.

> **Americans lose more of their property to civil asset forfeiture than they do to criminals**

## The War on Terror

As the American people watched the World Trade Center buildings collapse in New York City on September 11, 2001, they had no way of knowing that they would eventually forfeit some of their rights to their own government as a result, and pay a significant sum for the privilege. President George W. Bush coined the term "war on terrorism" just five days after the attacks, then "war on terror" a few days later. And that war has been with us every day since.

The domestic war on terror, including only expenditures for Homeland Security, has cost almost $700 billion since 2003.[13] The Transportation Security Administration (TSA) is Homeland Security's highest-profile enforcement arm. The TSA's mission statement is to "protect the nation's transportation systems to ensure freedom of movement for people and commerce." The TSA claims to be an "agile security agency, embodied by [*sic*] a professional workforce, that engages its partners and the American people to outmatch a dynamic threat," with the core values of "integrity, respect, and commitment."[14] To travelers familiar with its methods, these claims would be laughable were it not for the massive price tag and the indignation and humiliation travelers routinely suffer at the TSA's hands.

Of course, all the trouble might be worth it were the TSA effective. At first glance, it appears to be. The United States has not suffered another attack by air since September 2001. But the TSA is largely incompetent. Who says so? The TSA itself.

In tests Homeland Security performed to determine the TSA's effectiveness at rooting out potential attackers, the TSA failed to find planted weapons 95 percent of the time.[15] This is not terribly surprising to anyone who has passed through a TSA airport security line, where one typically encounters agents who range from chronically uninterested to vigilant to the point of unnatural personal enjoyment.

We all know enough of the history to know why and how things have come to this point. The case of Richard Reid, the so-called shoe bomber, is instructive. Reid boarded a plane bound for Miami in Paris just four months after the September 11 attacks. On that flight, he attempted to ignite explosives concealed in his shoes. Other passengers subdued him, and the plane was diverted to Logan International Airport in Boston, the closest U.S. airport. Reid was arrested, and in 2002 he pled guilty to eight federal counts of terrorism. He was sentenced to three life terms plus 110 years in prison.

Five years later, during which time no other terrorist attempted to bring down an American plane with explosives hidden in shoes, the TSA decided to force all American travelers to remove their shoes for security inspection. To this day, fliers continue to remove their shoes, unless they shell out $85 for TSA Pre-Check privileges.

The TSA has also banned liquids, including mashed potatoes and peanut butter, presumably because these can be assembled into or hide explosives. One assumes that were this danger a real concern, the TSA would not keep the confiscated liquids in a giant garbage can at the front of the security line. And although one bottle containing 35 ounces of liquid is potentially dangerous, apparently ten bottles of 3.5 ounces each are not.

However silly all of this might appear, the TSA has changed airport and travel culture. Many people, some high-profile, like Green Bay Packers wide receiver Trevor Davis, have been arrested at American airports for joking about bombs. And while we can all sleep better at night knowing that people with bad senses of humor find their way into the criminal justice system, the TSA has apprehended exactly no terrorists in its entire existence. For all of this, we pay more than $7 billion a year.

Worse, we have turned American citizens against one another with "If you see something, say something" campaigns. We have militarized local police departments, which results in an us-versus-them mentality that spills into many aspects of American life. We have raised a generation of children in a condition of generally unwarranted fear. We have also brought our troops, planes, and drones to many nations. And the killing we have done in those places, some warranted, some not, will doubtlessly result in the kind of hatred for the United States that led to the attacks that fired up this merry-go-round in the first place.

This is just the sort of thing we should expect when we go to war against a noun. Because "terror" cannot be adequately identified, it is not possible to know whether or when it has been extinguished. So the war goes on and on. President Barack

Obama seemed to sense as much in 2013, when in a speech at the National Defense University he announced a shift in policy that would see American efforts move away from "a boundless 'global war on terror'" to "a series of persistent, targeted efforts to dismantle specific networks of violent extremists that threaten America."[16] The Department of Homeland Security and its TSA kept right on going, though.

As if there were any doubt regarding the staying power of these irritants, politicians and activists persistently push to have the TSA secure surface transportation, too. So one of these days you will have to wait in an excruciatingly inefficient TSA line before boarding a bus, train, or ferry.

## War, What Is It Good For?

Absolutely nothing, according to Edwin Starr.[17] Starr wasn't exactly right, though. War is an effective tool in the hands of governments that would keep their own people under control. And Americans have been paying for three unwinnable wars for decades. These wars have grown the power of government at the expense of the people, and they have created seemingly permanent bureaucracies that do not have to accomplish anything to claim to be effective. In fact, they can secure ever more funding by being ineffective. We still have poverty, drugs, and terror, after all.

These sorts of wars are insidious on two levels. First, they either have always been or have come to be wars against American citizens. Because of these wars, Americans suffer under the yoke of authority, and they experience assaults on their rights and liberties. And, of course, Americans have to pick up the massive price tag on the wars, which have been more expensive than all of America's actual wars combined.

Second, there is no end in sight to any of these wars, nor can there be. There will be no D-Day, no V-J Day, no Treaty of Paris. All there will ever be is another demagogue promising to score a victory at great expense in money and citizens' liberties.

There will be only more coercion.

# 7

# TAXES

The American tax code is so complicated that no one can possibly understand every aspect of it. Not the taxpayers, who are obliged to follow it; nor legislators, who are charged with writing it; nor even the IRS, which is charged with enforcing it.

In fact, legislators cannot even agree on the length of the tax code! Their confusion is obvious:[1]

The income tax code and its associated regulations contain almost 5.6 million words—seven times as many words as the Bible. Taxpayers now spend about 5.4 billion hours a year trying to comply with 2,500 pages of tax laws.
—*Senator Rob Portman (R-OH)*

With its 6,000 pages and 500 million words, the complexity of our tax code is the prime source of frustration and anger felt by millions of Americans toward their government.

—*Representative Spencer Bachus (R–AL)*

The IRS tax code is 44,000 pages and growing.

—*Representative Walter Jones (R–NC)*

If these estimates are to be believed, the tax code is somewhere between 2,500 and 44,000 pages long, and contains between 5.6 million and 500 million words. The estimates vary so wildly that it seems our average legislator has no idea how long the tax code is.

If even those charged with writing the tax code do not know its length, how are we to abide by the incomprehensible mess they have created? When the federal income tax was introduced in 1913, the 1040 tax form came with only a single page of instructions. By 2012 that single page had become 189 pages. And another 500 forms accompany the 1040 we all know and love. Thank you, Washington, D.C.

It turns out those congressional guesstimates *underestimated* the size of the tax code. According to tax publisher CCH Inc., the federal tax code currently runs to more than 73,000 pages, more than three times the length it was in the 1970s. How big is 73,000 pages? If you were to print out the tax code, it would take up more than nine feet on a bookshelf. If someone were to work forty hours a week with no vacation, reading at a rate of one page every two minutes, he would read for a year. He would then learn that his hard work had been for nothing, as the code would have seen about 365 changes since he began reading. Between 2001 and 2016, Congress made nearly six thousand changes to the tax code, or about one every twenty-four hours.[2]

Because of all this complexity, the federal government established a position known as the National Taxpayer Advocate.

Nina Olson, who served in the role from 2001 to 2019, referred to the tax code's complexity as one of the most serious problems facing U.S. taxpayers. In her 2016 report to Congress, Olson noted that U.S. taxpayers and businesses spend about six billion hours a year complying with the filing requirements of the Internal Revenue Code. Those hours are the equivalent of one year's labor of three million full-time workers. This figure adds nothing to American productivity. It is wasted time.[3]

## Taxing for Social Engineering

So why has it come to this? The answer, unlike the tax code, is simple.

Politicians love social engineering, and they attempt to do it most often through the tax code. The government rewards preferred behaviors with tax breaks while punishing disapproved behaviors through rather arbitrary taxes. Proponents of using government authority this way call it "nudging." It really is coercion.

**If you were to print out the federal tax code, it would take up more than nine feet on a bookshelf**

Taxes designed to alter people's behavior are called *regulatory taxes*. Anyone who has purchased liquor or tobacco products is familiar with these. Whatever revenue regulatory taxes raise is of secondary importance. The primary purpose of a regulatory tax is to discourage the consumption or production of the taxed product. The government thinks you should smoke less, so it taxes tobacco heavily. In 2018 the average post-tax price of a pack of cigarettes in the United States reached $6.90, of which state and federal taxes accounted for $2.82.[4] The $2.82 tax represented almost 70 percent of the pre-tax retail price.[5] Studies have estimated that a tax on cigarettes that raises the price by 50 percent can be expected to reduce consumption of cigarettes by around 25 percent.[6]

One of the more recent behavior-changing taxes came with the Patient Protection and Affordable Care Act (ACA), commonly known as Obamacare. The government decided what people *should* do (have health insurance) and then passed legislation that would "encourage" them to do it by implementing a complex scheme of taxation.

This legislation did indeed change people's behaviors. The tax forced some people to purchase insurance—namely, those for whom qualifying insurance was less expensive than the tax. But it forced other people to *stop* purchasing insurance—namely, those for whom qualifying insurance was prohibitively expensive compared to the tax. The tax regulated some people into, and other people out of, the market for health insurance until it created a cycle of ever-increasing insurance prices.

This cycle resulted because of the economic phenomenon *adverse selection*. As healthy people leave the insurance market, the average health risk of the remaining pool of insured people rises. As the average health risk of the insured people rises, insurance companies must charge more for insurance. But raising the price of insurance increases the incentive for healthy people to drop their insurance coverage!

Why implement this regulation, then? Policy makers assume that people know whether they are "healthy" or "unhealthy" and that health is the only factor that matters in a person's decision to purchase insurance. These assumptions are incorrect, yet they form the basis for the ACA's requirement that everyone be insured. By forcing everyone to buy insurance, the argument goes, the price of insurance will be kept low. The ACA regulates the consumption of insurance by imposing a tax on the uninsured, thereby incenting people to purchase insurance to avoid the tax. The stated purpose of the tax is not to raise revenue (though it will do that) but to alter people's behaviors.

Similar examples abound for alcohol, fast food, sugary drinks, and other products. The government alters the behavior of its citizens as it sees fit by making certain behaviors much more expensive.

The flip side of the regulatory tax is the *subsidy*. When the government wants to encourage what it perceives to be desirable behaviors by making them less costly, it spends tax dollars to make desired behaviors more affordable for certain people. Various levels of government subsidize things like going to college, buying a house, and installing energy efficient windows.

## Taxing for Raising Revenue

Sometimes the government really is trying to increase its tax revenue, not just alter behavior. This was the case with the luxury tax imposed in 1991, a tax that would come back to haunt President George H. W. Bush, who had famously promised, "Read my lips: No new taxes."[7] In an attempt to raise taxes on the rich, the government imposed a 10 percent tax on things rich people buy: yachts, private planes, and expensive jewelry. At the time, Congress's Joint Committee on Taxation estimated that the luxury tax would generate $31 million in revenue in 1991.[8] But the tax actually produced only $16.6 million in revenue. Worse, the additional costs the federal government incurred because of the luxury tax resulted in a net *loss* of almost $8 million.[9]

What happened?

When the government taxes a product, the buyer and the seller of the product must share the tax burden. Buyers pay when business passes the tax on in the form of a higher sale price. Sellers pay by compensating their employees or suppliers less or by providing a lesser return to their owners and investors. Which party bears the greater burden depends on what economists call "elasticity"—that is, the extent to which a price increase reduces the buyer's desire to acquire the good, and the extent to which a profit decrease reduces the seller's desire to sell it.

Though the government did not intend the luxury tax to alter behavior, it did just that. Consumers cut back significantly on their purchases of luxury goods. Within twelve months of the government's levying the 10 percent tax, one-third of all American yacht builders had closed. The United States quickly went from being a net exporter of yachts to a net importer. The tax destroyed 7,600 jobs in the boating industry, plus another 1,470 in aircraft manufacturing and 330 in jewelry manufacturing. Those 9,400 jobs cost the government more than $24 million in lost income tax revenue and increased unemployment benefit expenses. Nor did the damage stop there. With less jewelry being made and fewer planes and yachts being built, the reduced demand for materials hurt the companies that supplied these industries. As the suppliers scaled back their operations, they laid off workers, too.[10]

Once again we see the unintended consequences of coercion.

Of course, not all markets react as strongly to taxes as did the yacht and private airplane markets. The more of a necessity a good is, the less strong the reaction to tax increases will be. When it comes to necessities like food and life-saving drugs, consumers tend to cut back on other things so they can continue to purchase the necessities that tax increases have made more expensive.

Notice that the government cannot actually raise taxes. What the government actually does is to raise tax *rates*. Taxes arise only after buyers and sellers in the economy react to the tax rates. As the 1991 luxury tax illustrates, an increase in tax rates does not necessarily result in an increase in tax revenue.

Think of the economy as a pie. The government chooses the *relative* size of its slice of the pie when it sets the tax rate. For example, the government may decide to take a 10 percent slice of the pie. But the *absolute* size of its slice, the tax revenue, depends on how large the pie is. A 10 percent slice of a six-inch pie will be smaller than a 10 percent slice of a twelve-inch pie. If the government raises tax rates but in response the economy shrinks, then the government ends up taking a larger slice of a smaller pie. Whether the government ends up with more pie depends on whether the pie shrank by less than the government's slice grew.

## Who Pays?

In 2016 American taxpayers paid 17.5 percent of their incomes to the federal government.[11] This includes all sources of income (wages, rental income, interest income, dividends, capital gains, inheritances, etc.) and all taxes paid to the federal government (income tax, Social Security tax, Medicare tax, capital gains tax, excise taxes, tariffs, etc.). The 2016 figure was no aberration: between 1951 and 2018, the amount taxpayers paid to the federal government fluctuated between 15.3 percent and 20 percent of income. And for three-quarters of that period, the figure fell somewhere between 16 percent and 18.5 percent.

The fact that the number has remained so stable is fascinating given that, over this same period, the top income tax rate ranged from a low of 28 percent to a high of 91 percent,[12] the top corporate profits tax ranged from a low of 35 percent to a high of almost 53 percent,[13] the capital gains tax rate ranged from a low of 15 percent to a high of almost 40 percent,[14] the top estate tax rate ranged from a low of 0 percent to a high of 77 percent,[15] and the payroll tax rate ranged from a low of 3 percent to a

high of 15.3 percent.[16] So for almost seventy years, it didn't matter whether the federal government taxed people or corporations, the rich or the working class, wage income or capital gains
income. And it didn't matter whether those tax rates were high
or low. Regardless of what and how much the federal government taxed, its total tax revenues remained at around 17 percent
of the economy.

Human behavior explains why the government's tax revenues
have not changed significantly. When the government raises tax
rates, people and businesses respond by altering their behaviors
to avoid the increased rates as best they can. For example, as
income tax rates rise, workers tend to prefer increased employer-
paid benefits (like health insurance and retirement contribu-
tions) to increased wages, because, unlike wages, employer-paid
benefits are not taxed. Warren Buffett, one of the world's richest
people, has for decades earned an annual salary of only $100,000
as chairman and CEO of Berkshire Hathaway.[17] But he earns
millions of dollars in stock options. Why? Because income he
earns in the form of salary is taxed at around 30 percent while
income he earns in the form of stock options is taxed at around
15 percent. Taxing one form of income at a higher rate than the
others causes people, where possible, to shift their incomes to
avoid the higher tax rate. This means that the government ends
up collecting less tax revenue than it anticipated when it raised
the tax rate.

Increased tax rates can lead to even more unintended consequences, not just decreased tax revenue. In 1944 the federal
government imposed a 30 percent "cabaret tax" on all receipts
at establishments that served food and allowed dancing or live
musical entertainment.[18] Entrepreneurs tried to get around the
law by allowing music only after food had been served and
cleared. The government stopped this approach by ruling that
to avoid the tax on meals, an establishment must make patrons

leave before the music began. Because the regulation exempted mechanical music from the tax, some establishments had performers lip-sync to records. The regulation also created an exemption for live instrumental music to which no one danced. Not coincidentally, the late 1940s saw a collapse in the popularity of big-band music—the sort to which people liked to dance—and a spike in the popularity of a new form of jazz, bebop, to which people did not dance. Certainly, changing tastes played a role, but at the very least the tax hastened the demise of the big-band era. In short, the tax had the effect, intended or not, of regulating the American music scene.

Obviously, people don't like paying more taxes. How do politicians regularly manage to raise tax rates if almost no one would vote for his own taxes to be raised? Politicians must look for scapegoats to tax, some minority who can easily be voted against. A popular group to target—both because they have lots of money and because they are a voting minority—is the rich. Many politicians cleverly combine their calls for raising taxes with a call for the rich to "pay their fair share." Conveniently, no politician has defined what constitutes "fair," so "fair" usually means "more."

The argument is that the rich take home the lion's share of income and use legions of tax attorneys and accountants to find ways around the tax law. But a look at the government's own data is instructive. According to a 2016 report from the Congressional Budget Office (CBO), the average household in the top 1 percent earned about $1.6 million in market income—that is, income derived from participation in the marketplace (wages, rental income, interest income, dividends, capital gains, inheritances, etc.). In the same year, the average middle-income household's market income was $53,000, and the market income for the average household among the poorest 20 percent was just under $16,000.[19] Even after tax lawyers and accountants did their legal and accounting acrobatics, the average household in the top 1 percent paid $544,000 in federal taxes (income, payroll, corporate, estate, capital gains, etc.). So the richest American households paid an average federal tax rate of 34 percent. The average middle-income household paid $8,900 in federal taxes, for an average tax rate of 17 percent.

Contrary to what we're told, then, the average middle-income American is not paying a higher tax rate than the richest Americans. In fact, the average middle-income American is paying *one-half* of the tax rate of the richest Americans. Let's look at it another way. The average household in the top 1 percent earns thirty times what the average middle-income household earns but pays more than sixty times the taxes.

What about the poorest 20 percent of households? The average household in this group paid $800 in federal taxes, for an average tax rate of 5 percent. In other words, the average richest household earned one hundred times what the average poorest household earned but paid almost seven hundred times the taxes.

One might argue that the rich *should* pay more than the middle class and the poor, but one cannot argue that the rich are paying less. The rich are not only paying more but are also paying *proportionally* more, and that's after applying all the deductions, exemptions, and loopholes.

But this isn't the end of the story. The government doesn't just tax. It also transfers. Instead of taking money from you, the government gives money to you. This isn't the same as a tax rebate. If you pay more tax than you should have, then when you file your taxes you receive the overage back. With a tax rebate, the government isn't giving you money; it is correcting an error wherein you gave the government too much money. By contrast, with a transfer, the government actually gives you money in exchange for nothing. Examples of transfers include the Earned Income Tax Credit, supplemental income payments for the poor, Social Security retirement benefits, and disability benefits.[20]

The question of who is not paying his "fair share" of taxes becomes very interesting when we look at taxes and transfers. The table below shows the average household market income (in 2013) for American households divided into various income categories, as reported by the CBO.[21] The tables show gross income, before taxes and transfers, coming from all market sources: labor, interest income, rental income, business income, capital gains, inheritance, and so on. The "bottom quintile" is the poorest 20 percent of households. The "second quintile" is the next-to-the-poorest 20 percent of households. The "middle quintile" is the solidly middle class. The "fourth quintile" can be considered upper-middle class. After this point, the CBO breaks the households down into smaller sets. The final set is the "Top 1 percent," the richest 1 percent of American households (where "rich" is defined by income, not by wealth).

| Household Income Category | Market Income |
|---|---|
| Bottom Quintile | $15,800 |
| Second Quintile | $31,300 |
| Middle Quintile | $53,000 |
| Fourth Quintile | $88,700 |
| 81 percent to 90 percent | $135,000 |
| 91 percent to 95 percent | $189,000 |
| 96 percent to 99 percent | $317,000 |
| Top 1 percent | $1,562,000 |

Now let's see how much (on average) these households paid in federal taxes (all federal taxes combined) and how much they received in transfers in 2013.

The same CBO report shows the following:[22]

| Household Income Category | Market Income | Transfers | Federal Taxes | Average Tax Rate (ignoring transfers) |
|---|---|---|---|---|
| Bottom Quintile | $15,800 | $9,600 | $800 | 5.1% |
| Second Quintile | $31,300 | $16,200 | $4,000 | 12.8% |
| Middle Quintile | $53,000 | $16,700 | $8,900 | 16.8% |
| Fourth Quintile | $88,700 | $15,000 | $17,600 | 19.8% |
| 81 percent to 90 percent | $135,000 | $12,100 | $30,400 | 22.5% |
| 91 percent to 95 percent | $189,000 | $12,400 | $46,200 | 24.4% |
| 96 percent to 99 percent | $317,000 | $9,800 | $86,000 | 27.1% |
| Top 1 percent | $1,562,000 | $9,600 | $534,100 | 34.2% |

Using this information, let's calculate the average effective tax rate for each group after accounting for government transfers. The results are shown in the table on the next page.

Two remarkable results emerge. First, even if we ignore transfers, the top 1 percent are being taxed at around twice the rate of the middle class (34 percent versus 17 percent), and at almost seven times the rate of the poorest 20 percent (34 percent versus 5 percent). Second, when we include transfers, only the richest 40 percent are paying any federal taxes at all. The middle class and poor receive more money back from the federal government in transfers than they pay to it in taxes. These are not statutory marginal tax rates (i.e., the tax rates stated in the law that apply to specific income ranges) but average effective tax rates (i.e., the fraction of their incomes people actually pay).

| Household Income Category | Market Income | Taxes Less Transfers | Average Effective Tax Rate (including transfers) |
| --- | --- | --- | --- |
| Bottom Quintile | $15,800 | –$8,800 | –55.7% |
| Second Quintile | $31,300 | –$12,200 | –39.0% |
| Middle Quintile | $53,000 | –$7,800 | –14.7% |
| Fourth Quintile | $88,700 | $2,600 | 2.9% |
| 81 percent to 90 percent | $135,000 | $18,300 | 13.6% |
| 91 percent to 95 percent | $189,000 | $33,800 | 17.9% |
| 96 percent to 99 percent | $317,000 | $76,200 | 24.0% |
| Top 1 percent | $1,562,000 | $524,500 | 33.6% |

These results also help us understand the debate between those who say the government should cut taxes and those who say that tax cuts are really tax cuts for the rich. If the correct way to think about transfers is as a negative tax—that is, transfers are simply tax reductions—then pretty much any tax cut is a tax cut for the rich, because, on average, the rich are the only people paying federal taxes at all.

Each year, a Gallup poll asks whether various income groups are paying their "fair share" in taxes. In April 2019, 17 percent of respondents said that lower-income people were paying too little, 7 percent said that middle-income people were paying too little, and 62 percent said that upper-income people were paying too little.[23] These results probably reflect people's misconceptions about how much others pay. In a University of Michigan study, economist Joel Slemrod found that 51 percent of survey respondents thought that middle-income families pay a higher average tax rate than do high-income families.[24] Remember, the average tax rate on middle-income families is *half* that on upper-income families—and this is *after* accounting for deductions, exemptions, other accounting gymnastics, and ignoring transfers.[25]

> **Once we account for transfers, only the richest 40 percent of Americans pay any federal taxes at all**

These figures reflect the fact that the United States has a progressive tax system: a system in which tax rates increase as income increases. One argument against a progressive tax system is that there is no obvious "fair" tax. It is unclear whether requiring the rich to pay a rate twice that of the middle class is more or less fair than requiring the rich to pay a rate three times that of the middle class. A flat tax would eliminate the need to determine a "fair" rate: everyone, regardless of income level, would pay the same percentage of his income. The rich would pay a greater *amount* than the poor, but everyone would pay the same percentage of income.

Another argument against a progressive tax system also applies against a flat tax system: people share equally in government services. The rich drive on the same roads as the poor. They have the same public schools available to them. The military defends them just as much as it does the poor. The belief that people are equal under the law suggests that they should also pay equally for the protection the law affords. Perhaps a "fair" tax is one that charges the same dollar amount to each person, like a standard bill for government services, regardless of income.

Again, we cannot know what "fair" means, but it is clear that politicians use the rich as scapegoats, against whom they unite low- and middle-income voters, for their own gain in the form of more tax revenue. This seems unfair.


## No Solutions

Every budgetary cycle, politicians plead with voters to allow them to increase tax rates, arguing that they need the additional tax revenues to balance the budget. But politicians tend not to use increased revenues to balance the budget. What they do instead is increase spending, initiating a never-ending cycle: increased spending requires increased tax rates, which enables increased spending, which requires increased tax rates, and on and on.

When the government spends more money than it takes in, it needs to borrow money. This deficit spending has become the norm. In fact, in the sixty years from 1961 through 2019, the federal government never balanced its budget. Even in the four years during the Clinton administration for which official debt figures showed budget surpluses, the federal debt actually increased.[26]

Still, deficit spending becomes politically unpopular sometimes. In those cases, politicians argue that they should be allowed to spend more and that the additional spending should be financed by "the rich."

But the math simply doesn't work. In 2018 the federal budget deficit approached $800 billion.[27] To balance the budget, the government would need to tax the top 1 percent at almost a 100 percent average tax rate. Of course, we could do this only once, since a 100 percent tax rate would eliminate the top 1 percent from society. In the next year, with the top 1 percent gone, the government would have to impose a near 100 percent tax on the top 5 percent to balance the budget. This would eliminate the top 5 percent from society. Very quickly, the government would run out of people to tax.

This example is extreme—no one is advocating imposing a 100 percent tax on the rich.[28] But it illustrates the point that even with historically unprecedented tax rates, there aren't enough rich taxpayers to keep the federal budget in balance.

Consider a more realistic case. In 2019 the federal deficit exceeded $1 trillion, and federal receipts from all sources combined reached $3.3 trillion. Even if raising taxes had no detrimental effects on productivity, to balance the budget would require raising all tax rates by one-third. The lowest income tax bracket would rise from 10 percent to 13 percent. Social Security and Medicare payroll taxes would rise from 12.4 percent to 16.1 percent. The top income tax rate would rise from almost 40 percent to 52 percent. All other federal taxes, tariffs, and fees would similarly rise by one-third. This would be a historically unprecedented increase in tax rates. Yet it would merely balance the budget.

But raising taxes does reduce productivity. So balancing the budget would require a substantially greater increase in tax rates than a mere one-third to offset the lost productivity.

Everywhere one looks when considering taxes, one sees the knowledge problem in full operation. The U.S. economy is simply too complex for politicians to adjust it effectively by fiddling with the tax code. When politicians try, they fail—and they typically make matters worse. And when politicians do not collect the money they thought they would, they go right on spending anyway. Over the years they learned that voters would not hold them accountable if they ran debt levels to ever more dizzying heights, so that is precisely what they did. We have reached the point now where the debt has become so large, it is a problem that is mathematically impossible to solve.

# 8

# DEBT

Remember that time you wanted to buy something but you realized you could not afford it so you put it back on the shelf? That's the biggest difference between you and the federal government.

Unlike you, the government rarely considers what it can afford. When politicians do hesitate to spend, it is more because of concern about how deficit spending will affect the next election than because they see the dangers of deficit spending. How do we know this? Because in almost every election, candidates from both parties campaign on fiscal discipline, and then, regardless of which party wins, the deficits continue.

In short, the federal government is throwing the biggest party in history, and it will stick your children and grandchildren with history's biggest bar tab.

How bad is it? In 2019 the amount the federal government officially owed passed $22 trillion. Of this, the government had borrowed more than $16 trillion from private individuals, companies, and foreign governments. It borrowed another $5.9 trillion from federal agencies and government programs that have run surpluses—largely from the Social Security trust fund.[1] As a result, there was no money in the Social Security trust fund. There never had been. The "trust fund" amounts to a big, fat IOU from Uncle Sam.

You might have heard that the trillions borrowed from Social Security doesn't count as debt, because it is money that government has borrowed from itself. This would be great, but it overlooks one very important fact: ultimately, the government doesn't owe the money to itself. It owes the money to current and future retirees. True, the government could, legally speaking, cut or even eliminate Social Security benefits. But the legal facts are irrelevant to the economic facts. The economic facts are that most people believe the government owes them the promised benefits, so most of them are right now choosing how much to save and how much to consume on the assumption that they will receive the promised money.

So $22 trillion it is.

But what is $22 trillion anyway? There are so many zeroes on these numbers that people just tune out when they hear them. Maybe this will help. If you made $50,000 a year, you would have to work for 440 million years to earn $22 trillion.

Maybe that doesn't help so much after all. How about this: 22 trillion drops of water would fill about 575 Olympic-sized swimming pools.[2]

Still too fantastic? Think of it this way instead: if blades of grass were dollars, it would take more than 66,000 football fields (including both end zones) to contain enough grass to get to $22 trillion.[3]

Let's try this instead: if you were to go to Germany and buy every item, on every shelf, in every store, in every city in the entire country, it would not cost you $22 trillion. In fact, if you added all the things in all the stores in all the cities in all of Italy, you still wouldn't be there. As it goes, you would have to buy every single thing for sale—both goods and services—in all the stores in all of *Europe* over an entire year to approach $22 trillion.

## The Government Owes Much More Than the Debt

If these exercises haven't made things more comprehensible, you won't like what comes next. Because as bad as $22 trillion is, it is only a small part of the picture.

The federal government has promised retirement and medical benefits to current and future retirees that it doesn't and won't have the money to cover—even after accounting for future

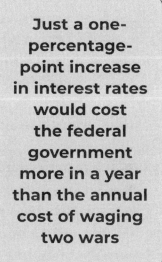

**Just a one-percentage-point increase in interest rates would cost the federal government more in a year than the annual cost of waging two wars**

tax revenues. These promised future payments that the government won't be able to cover are called *unfunded obligations* and are classified separately from "official debt."

With unfunded obligations, the government has promised all kinds of money to people that it has no legal obligation to pay. Where Social Security is concerned, this is especially distressing. The story Americans have been told since its inception is that a Social Security retirement account is safe, that the money will be there when they reach retirement age. Social Security is better than private retirement accounts, we have been told, because the money in a private retirement account is subject to the vagaries of the marketplace. One bad turn in the market and you could lose everything just when you needed it most. Social Security retirement accounts, on the other hand, are supposedly safe because Social Security invests only in U.S. Treasury Bills, and U.S. Treasury Bills are backed by the full faith and credit of the U.S. government.[4] This is true, but as with everything the government says, you should take it with a grain of salt. It is most certainly not the *whole* truth. Although the law requires the Social Security trust fund to invest your Social Security taxes only in Treasury Bills, no law requires the Social Security trust fund to give you your money back. At any time, Congress can decide that it just isn't going to pay your Social Security (or Medicare) benefits, promised or not. Because the government isn't legally obligated to pay you your benefits, the promised benefits are classified as *obligations* rather than as *debt*. Isn't that clever?

Estimating unfunded obligations—how much the government has promised but will not be able to pay—is difficult because it involves estimating future interest rates, future population growth rates, future tax rates, future economic growth, and a host of other things that require complicated guesswork. Estimates of unfunded obligations vary widely, but even the lowest estimate is huge. As of 2017, the estimates ranged from around $50 trillion to more than $200 trillion.[5] Even if we take a conservative estimate of $80 trillion, that number matches the economic output of the entire planet in 2017.[6]

To spend $80 trillion, you would need to buy all the goods and services for sale on the entire planet for an entire year. And that's for a *conservative* estimate.

## Three Problems

That magnitude of debt and unfunded obligations causes three immediate problems. First, it allows politicians to make much ado about nothing. In February 2011, faced with rising voter concern about the deficit, the Obama administration proposed cutting $300 million in community block grants.[7] Opponents said that the block grants helped the neediest Americans and that such a huge cut would devastate the people who needed government assistance the most. For several weeks politicians and pundits publicly debated the proposed $300 million cut. To be sure, $300 million is a huge sum of money, but relative to the size of federal spending, it is almost nothing. The year Obama suggested the cuts, the federal government spent more than $3.6 trillion, or about $300 million every forty-five minutes.[8] In the time it took politicians to decide to cut that $300 million, the government spent around seven hundred times that amount. The numbers are so large that politicians can appear to make meaningful cuts while actually doing nothing.

The second problem is that perpetually low interest rates are necessary to keep this financial house of cards standing. The Federal Reserve, which is theoretically an independent body, controls the money supply, which, in turn, affects interest rates. But the thing to remember is that the Fed was created by Congress, can be dissolved by Congress, must report annually to the House of Representatives, and is run by people appointed by the President and confirmed by the Senate. In the real world, the Fed is not even close to independent. It is without question subject to political pressures.

A truly independent Federal Reserve might be inclined to serve the interests of the American people, but political pressures push the Fed to serve the interests of Washington. And what does Washington want? Low interest rates. When politicians argue for lower interest rates, they do everything they can to make it look like they care only about you. They typically point to lower mortgage rates for homeowners and lower student loan rates for college students. Although lower interest rates are clearly good for borrowers, they are not good for everyone. Low interest rates hurt people who are saving or, worse yet, living off their savings. But you won't hear politicians talk about these people all that often.

You also won't hear them talk about how the single largest beneficiary of low interest rates is the federal government itself. In 2019 the federal government paid around 2.5 percent annual interest on its debt.[9] The historical average since World War II has been around 6 percent.[10] With $22 trillion in official debt, just a one-percentage-point increase in interest rates would cost the federal government an additional $220 billion annually in interest expense alone. How much is $220 billion? That is much more than the peak annual cost of the Iraq and Afghanistan wars.[11]

More disturbingly, if the interest rate the government paid on its debt rose to its historical average of 6 percent, the annual interest expense alone would exceed $1 trillion. This forces the Federal Reserve to weigh the trade-off between guarding against inflation by allowing interest rates to rise and guarding against government insolvency by holding interest rates low.

The third problem we face from so much debt is that we are quickly approaching a point of no return. The $22 trillion federal debt exceeded the entire annual economic output (GDP) of the United States, which reached $20 trillion in 2018. The federal government owes more than all Americans and American companies earn in an entire year—combined. This comparison of a government's debt to the country's economy is called the debt-to-GDP ratio. While eye-opening, the ratio can be misleading for two reasons. First, the government doesn't own the GDP. The GDP belongs to the people. It is, after all, the combined incomes of all the people and companies in the country. Second, from a practical perspective, the debt really doesn't matter. What matters is the government's ability to *service* the debt—that is, to make the annual interest payments. How much debt you have on your credit card, practically speaking, doesn't matter. What matters is that you can afford to make your minimum monthly payments. As long as you can do that, you remain in good financial standing.

The appropriate measure of a government's ability to service its debt is the debt-to-receipts ratio. Federal *receipts* are all sources of federal government income combined: taxes, fees, tariffs, and everything else. In 2019 federal receipts totaled $3.3 trillion, making the federal government's debt nearly seven times the federal government's income.[12] For perspective, that's like a household with a $60,000 annual income being $400,000 in debt. But this debt is not like a $400,000 mortgage, where you have an asset to sell off if times get tough. This is like credit card debt, which you accumulate by living beyond your means. All you have in the end is a mammoth bill and a bigger headache.

And this ignores the trillions in unfunded obligations. Adding unfunded obligations, even at the conservative $50 trillion estimate, puts the government's total debt and unfunded obligations at nearly twenty-two times the federal government's receipts. That's like the parents with $60,000 in household income owing $400,000 on their credit cards and promising to pay for their two children, plus nine of their friends, to attend private colleges. Oh, and the parents have saved nothing toward those promises.

This is where the debt story becomes truly alarming. To service more than $70 trillion in debt plus unfunded obligations at a 2.5 percent annual interest rate, the government would need to make annual interest payments of about $2 trillion. But the government doesn't have $2 trillion to put toward interest payments. Recent budgets have provided only about one-tenth of that amount. The government can do nothing to come up with

$2 trillion, save permanently shutting down about half of everything it does.

In other words, it is a mathematical certainty that the federal government is going to default, sooner or later, on at least some of its financial obligations.

Look at Social Security. Since 2010, the Social Security trust fund has collected less money in payroll taxes than it pays out in benefits. Interest on the trust fund has made up the difference. But the Social Security Board of Trustees, in its 2019 annual report, projected that annual expenses would exceed payroll taxes and the annual interest starting in 2020.[13] Once costs exceed total income, the trust fund will need to draw down its reserves to keep paying promised benefits. The Board of Trustees reported that the trust fund would be depleted by 2035. So according to the government's own estimates, Social Security will be bankrupt in less than two decades.

How can Social Security avoid insolvency? The Board of Trustees estimated that either retirees would need to take an "immediate and permanent" 17 percent to 20 percent cut in benefits (depending on whether the cuts applied to all retirees or just those retiring after 2019), workers would have to pay 22 percent more in payroll taxes, or the government would need to impose some combination of cuts and taxes. Keep in mind, these projections are from *the federal government itself.*

## Running Out of Options

Few things put the fear of God into politicians like voter outrage at the federal deficit and the long-term debt it brings. So as the people become irritated by deficits and debt, politicians buy them off, providing ever more government handouts as we careen toward the fiscal abyss. The pressure is always to give the people more while asking them to pay less, and debt is the magic elixir that makes this possible.

Congress has always limited the amount of money the federal government can borrow (although prior to World War I, Congress approved borrowing only for specific purposes rather than for funding the general budget).[14] But the debt limit is a fiction. Congress sets all federal spending, so Congress decides whether it gets to spend more than it earns, and by how much. We see how this will play out: Congress will increase the debt limit that it imposed on itself when it is politically expedient to do so. And it is always expedient to spend more on constituents, what with elections and all.

From 1962 to 2011, Congress raised the debt ceiling seventy-four times.[15] That's an average of once every eight months for a half century. This isn't a ceiling; it is a low-hanging mist.

And with good reason. The federal government's declaring bankruptcy is not an option. It would create unprecedented financial turmoil worldwide and lead to the collapse of the federal government. Nor is servicing all the debt and unfunded obligations a realistic option. Remember, to service $70 trillion, the federal government must come up with about $2 trillion annually, in addition to all the money it currently collects. The most common approaches to addressing deficits, raising taxes and cutting spending, aren't viable solutions, either: one because of mathematics, the other because of politics.

The longer the government puts off raising the money it needs, the more money it will have to raise when it finally gets around to doing so. Even if the government decided to tackle the issue tomorrow, raising taxes across the board wouldn't be a good option. To come up with an additional $2 trillion a year, the government would have to raise taxes on every person and every company by almost 70 percent. And that assumes the 70 percent tax hike created no drag on the economy. If, as is certain, people adjusted their behaviors by working less, moving their investments abroad, and starting fewer businesses, then the government would have to raise taxes by significantly more than 70 percent to come up with the extra money.

Raising taxes on corporations isn't a good option either. Corporations don't actually pay taxes; they collect taxes from customers in the form of higher prices, from workers and suppliers in the form of lower wages and payments, and from investors and owners in the form of lower returns. Politicians talk about taxing corporations because voters will support such taxes while remaining largely unaware that they are actually supporting taxes on themselves.

> **Imagine you make $60,000 a year but owe $400,000 on your credit cards and have promised to put eleven people through college:** *that* **is what the federal government's finances are like**

Raising taxes on the rich isn't an option because there aren't enough rich people to tax. In 2013 (the latest year for which data were available), the top 1 percent of income earners earned a total of $1.7 trillion.[16] Even a 100 percent tax on the rich wouldn't raise enough money to service the government's financial obligations for one year. And were the government to confiscate 100 percent of the rich's income, many of the rich would leave the country. So we'd see the same pattern we observed in the previous chapter: in only a few short years, the government would run out of people to tax. It would move from the top 1 percent to the top 3 or 4 percent, and soon it would come after the middle class and the poor.

Politicians routinely say we can "grow" our way out of our debt problem. It is true that as the economy grows, so too do tax revenues. But you know what happens when the government takes in more money? Politicians spend it all. And then they spend more. Since 1950, for every additional dollar the government has brought in as tax revenue in one year, it has spent an additional $1.28 the following year.[17] Historically, bringing in more money seems to make the problem worse, not better.

Which brings us to the political implications of the debt.

If the laws of mathematics prevent the government from raising an additional $2 trillion annually, the laws of politics prevent it from cutting $2 trillion in spending. As we saw in the previous chapter, a majority of voters are net recipients of government largesse. People in the bottom three income quintiles (on average) receive more money back in tax credits than they pay in taxes.[18] In clearer language: about 60 percent of voters directly benefit from increased government spending, because more government spending means they receive more services and transfers for which they don't pay. If almost a supermajority of voters benefits from increased spending, then it is extremely unlikely that politicians will cut that spending significantly. Politicians found it difficult to cut $300 million in community block grants, and that was only one-hundredth of 1 percent of federal spending. A $2 trillion cut is almost seven thousand times larger. And no, a combination of higher taxes and spending cuts is not going to work either. The taxes and cuts required are both so large that, even when employed together, they are mathematically and politically unfathomable.

If the government cannot come up with $2 trillion annually through either increased taxation or reduced spending, and if outright bankruptcy is not an option, then only two options remain. Both are going to happen.

The first is that the government will at least partially default on its unfunded obligations. Politicians will hide behind the technicality that obligations aren't, legally, the same as debt, so they can correctly say that the government is not declaring bankruptcy. Of course, to the people who were promised the money, the government's refusal to pay up will look exactly like bankruptcy. Politicians will attempt to divert people's anger by saying things like:

> It isn't fair that some people had the good fortune to work for employers who provided private retirement accounts while others did not. Those people don't need Social Security at all. When Social Security was created, it was never intended for them. It was intended as a safety net for the poorest workers. Until now, Social Security has collected enough money that it could extend benefits to everyone, even those who didn't need them. But we can no longer afford to waste Social Security money supplementing lavish retirements for the rich. Therefore, the privileged few who are fortunate enough to have private retirement accounts will see their Social Security benefits reduced so that we can maintain full benefits for less fortunate workers—the workers for whom Social Security was really intended.

As they have done many times in the past, politicians will try to make their inability to manage the country's finances look like the fault of the rich preying on the poor. While we fight among ourselves, the real culprits will get off the hook.

Cutting Social Security benefits for workers who have private retirement accounts will not be enough. The government will simply print the rest of the money that it needs. The current euphemism is *quantitative easing*. The Federal Reserve prints more money and then hands it over to the federal government. But when the Fed pumps money into the economy, prices rise. Prices have risen so much as a result of this that a U.S. dollar in 2019 bought less than what a U.S. quarter bought in 1975.[19] In 1975 the money supply amounted to $273 billion.[20] In 2019 it reached $3.8 trillion. So the U.S. money supply grew by more than a factor of ten, while the quantity of goods and services produced in the United States merely tripled.[21] And the population rose only by half.[22] Why does this matter?

Money gets its value from the things it can buy. You perceive a $20 bill to be valuable only because people will give you goods and services you want in exchange for it. Absent those goods and services, the $20 bill is worthless. The more goods and services there are relative to the number of dollars that exist, the more valuable each of those dollars is. The fewer goods and services there are relative to the number of dollars that exist, the less valuable each of those dollars is. Every time the government increases the money in circulation, the money in your pocket loses value. As your money loses value, you need more of it to buy the same number of goods and services. This is inflation. And it is the government's fault.

The Federal Reserve sets the money supply. The Fed could have held the money supply constant, as it was forced to do when United States followed the gold standard. Instead, it grew the money supply faster than the quantity of goods and services grew, and now our dollars buy far less than they once did. This is what happens when the Fed serves Washington's interests instead of yours.

Now here's the interesting catch. Inflation doesn't occur immediately when the Fed prints new money. It occurs after the new money has begun to circulate in the economy. If you are lucky enough to be one of the first to spend the newly printed dollars, then you get to spend them when they are still worth more. After those new dollars begin to circulate, prices rise and everyone's dollars begin to lose their value. Guess who gets to spend the new dollars first? That's right, the federal government.

At this point it should be clear that inflation is identical to a tax. When the government taxes you, it takes a portion of

your money. When the Fed prints new money, it takes a portion of your money's purchasing power. Although you might be
able to avoid some taxes, it isn't easy to avoid inflation. If the
government taxes cigarettes, you can choose not to smoke. If it
taxes wages, you can accept a lower wage in exchange for more
(untaxed) employer-paid benefits. But when the Fed prints more
money, all dollars everywhere lose some of their value. The only
way to avoid this tax is not to hold dollars at all. As you might
imagine, this is nearly impossible.

And what might happen if the Fed does for the next sixty
years what it did over the past sixty? What cost $1 in 1975 cost
almost $5 in 2019. If the same trend continues, what cost $5 in
2019 will cost $50 by 2070 or so. Somewhere along the way,
dollars will lose all meaning, just as pennies have now. Imagine
a "need a dollar, take a dollar" container at the convenience store
counter. When this comes to pass, it will be a very short step
for politicians to propose a "new dollar." The rhetoric will go
something like this:

> Because of irresponsible bankers and an unregulated finan-
> cial sector run amok, your hard-earned dollars aren't worth
> what they once were. Remember when a dollar would buy
> you a gallon of gas? We need to return to those days when
> the dollar was strong. To achieve this, Congress is instruct-
> ing the Federal Reserve to issue the New American Dollar.
> These new dollars will be worth more than the old dollars,
> and all Americans will be required to exchange their old
> dollars for the new.

A century of irresponsibility will be whitewashed, and regular American citizens will be left holding the same empty bag.

Sadly, there is precedent for such nonsense. Prior to 1933,
U.S. currency included a lot of gold coins and certificates

redeemable in gold. With the Emergency Banking Act of 1933, Congress authorized the Secretary of the Treasury to confiscate Americans' gold certificates, gold coins, and gold bullion if, in his judgment, "such action is necessary to protect the currency system of the United States."[23] Following the Emergency Banking Act, the government confiscated Americans' gold and replaced it with new currency that was not redeemable in gold.

## Insidious Coercion

> Debt is an especially insidious form of coercion—one imposed on citizens who haven't even been born

The federal debt has reached such a staggering level that at least some of these negative outcomes seem unavoidable. But there is a way to stop the problem from getting any worse.

Between 2000 and 2018, the U.S. economy (as measured by nominal GDP) grew at an average annual rate of 4 percent.[24] Historically, the federal government's total receipts have averaged about 17 percent of GDP.[25] If the economy continued to grow at 4 percent per year and the federal government held spending constant for five years—not even adjusting for inflation—then within those five years the government would have its first balanced budget since the Eisenhower administration.[26] From that point forward, the federal government could again increase spending as long as it never increased it faster than the economy grew.

The catch is that politicians don't like reducing planned spending *increases*, let alone holding spending constant. Since 1964, only once has the federal government spent less in one year than it did the year before—and that was in 2010, immediately after the year of stimulus spending intended to help pull us out of the Great Recession. For this plan to work, politicians would have to hold spending constant for five years. That means forgoing about $4.5 trillion in spending.

As extreme as this solution is, it is the only thing that stands between the federal government and effective bankruptcy. Five years of systematic belt tightening will be difficult, but the misery that will result from business as usual will make the Great Depression look like a weekend bender. It would have been better to address these problems decades ago. Now we cannot solve our financial problems. The best we can do is to stop them from getting worse. Only after we learn to live within our means can we turn our attention to making good on the promises we have made to present and future retirees. Sometime after that, maybe, we can think about actually paying down our debt.

In a self-governing republic, we can spend our money any way we see fit, even if doing so is a terrible idea. But that is not what we are doing. When the government borrows money to spend on people today, it is forcing future generations either to repay that money or to make interest payments on it forever. This is an especially insidious form of coercion, because the government coerces citizens who have absolutely no say in the matter. The coerced citizens cannot vote, or even speak out, because they have not yet been born. When they arrive, a crippling debt with no means of repayment will be their sad birthright.

This is as far afield as we could have gotten from the preamble of the U.S. Constitution, which made clear that the Constitution was designed to "secure the Blessings of Liberty to ourselves and our Posterity."

# 9

# BUSYBULLIES

In addition to the knowledge problem and the problems of human nature, another problem emerges in the normal course of human business that causes all kinds of mischief. People tend to like to boss other people around. Bossiness may well be an aspect of human nature, but it combines with other things in so pernicious a way that it deserves its own discussion.

When we ask the government to use its coercive power to solve a problem, government expands. For the government to do more requires that it have more resources, which means more taxes and more authority, which means more coercion. Over time, repeatedly turning to the government to fix things causes government's reach to grow from adjudicating disputes, to preventing people from harming one another, to dictating how people should live their lives more generally.

This last step marks a qualitative change in what we have come to expect from government. In the first two steps, government acts as an umpire. Its role is to ensure that people don't harm one another and to attain redress for the harmed when they do. But in the third step, government moves from refereeing cooperation among people to directing their solitary actions. We generally refer to this as regulation, but whatever we call it, it is the government telling people how to live their lives.

Almost no part of our lives is free from regulation by some level of government, if not multiple levels. Government has its hands in everything, from the mundane—the contents of our mattresses, the flow of water in our showers, the quality of the ingredients we use to make our coffee, the construction of our coffee makers, and on and on—to what chemicals we may put in our bodies, to whom we may marry, to what possessions we may leave to others when we die.

Early on, children learn a word for people who tell others how to live their lives: busybodies.

As long as humans have lived in communities, there have been busybodies—people who think they know how others should live their lives. Busybodies turn their noses up at you when they see you smoking. They raise their eyebrows when you say that you have more than one drink a night. They wag their fingers and lecture you about exercise when you put on weight.

Until the past century, the primary tool of busybodies was social stigma. They shamed people. But as government has grown in power and scope, busybodies have found a better way to satisfy their need to mind everyone else's business. They harness the coercive power of government. Like a game character leveling up, busybodies become busybullies when they meet government.

In most cases when voters contemplate government action, they agree on the ends: less poverty, less crime, and less pollution are generally desirable, as are more employment, more opportunities, and more safety. Voter disagreements largely center on the means to achieve those ends. We end up with some people arguing for an increased minimum wage because $10 an hour is better than $7, and other people arguing against an increased minimum because $7 an hour is better than $0. Both sides agree on the end: minimum wage workers should be helped, or at least not harmed. They differ on the best way to achieve that end.

Where busybullies are involved, though, disputes about appropriate policy are no longer disputes about alternate means to an agreed end. Disputes are about the end itself—specifically, how people should live their lives. From prostitution to marijuana to tobacco, even to raising our own children, busybullies use the power of government to bully others into submission.

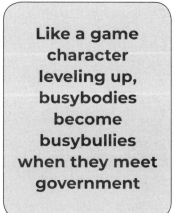

**Like a game character leveling up, busybodies become busybullies when they meet government**

Don't like pornography? Pressure the government to declare it a public health crisis.

Don't like marijuana? Demand that the government ruin the lives of those who use it.

Don't think children should play outside unattended? Have the government take them away from their parents.

Busybodies have always disapproved of others' choices. But today, as busybullies, they use the government to force others to comply with their worldview.

## What Lies Beneath Busybullying

Two flawed beliefs lie at the root of busybullying. First, the busybully implicitly assumes that humans are homogeneous—that we all share (or should share) the same preferences, priorities, expectations, beliefs, and values. Because the busybully doesn't enjoy drinking alcohol, he assumes that no reasonable person would. Because the busybully doesn't see the point in owning a gun, he assumes that there is no point. Because the busybully is disgusted at the thought of sex for money, he believes that everyone else should be disgusted by it, too. In short, the busybully sees his view of the world as the correct one and alternate views as flawed.

Second, the busybully doesn't believe in equality under the law, or that any particular form of tolerance is a virtue. Instead, he believes that where his views regarding what is good and proper differ from those of others, the government should impose his views on everyone else. He will convince himself that this is a matter not of opposing views but of truth and error, ignoring the fact that the right to hold an opinion is not contingent on that opinion's being correct. The problem, of course, is that he does not admit that he might not be in possession of the truth, that the knowledge problem might be playing out before his eyes. He will, for example, support laws prohibiting people from buying nonessentials on Sundays, because he considers it a fact that people should be spending that day in church, not consuming things they don't need. And he always seems to know what others need. More important, he never senses that he might be trading in opinion, which might well be incorrect, and not in fact.

Busybullies combine moral superiority, zeal, and political activism to direct the government to regulate others' behavior according to their points of view. You will conform, or you will be fined, jailed, or both. To assuage what limited remorse they might feel, they typically invoke the mantra of "public health, safety, and welfare."

Look at their recent foray into e-cigarettes. Busybullies claim to be acting in the interest of public health, but when you point out that people use e-cigarettes to quit smoking—a more dangerous activity—busybullies respond by claiming that the real problem is that e-cigarettes are dangerous to others. When presented with evidence that e-cigarettes are actually less dangerous than cigarettes, and less dangerous than many other things people are already doing voluntarily, like drinking to excess or leading a sedentary life, the busybullies say that, no, the real problem is that e-cigarettes are "dangerous to youth."[1] For perspective, in 2017 more than 850,000 Americans died of heart disease, 47,000 from suicide, 4,500 from medical errors, and 3,700 from drowning, but fewer than 35 died from vaping—and those deaths were caused not by the vaping itself but by tainted e-liquids.[2] Of course, every life lost is a cause for concern, but it seems reasonable that for something to be declared a public health problem, it should be somewhere near the top of the list of things that kill people. In response to data, busybullies offer anecdotes but no compelling evidence, because, in their eyes, moral superiority is its own evidence. Any evidence presented in opposition to their claims, however, they subject to the highest scrutiny.

A perfect case in point: Thomas Ylioja, a "smoking cessation expert," has commented on survey data on e-cigarette use by teenagers, claiming, "We have a whole generation of young people who are addicted to these products."[3] Surgeon General Jerome Adams uses the same rationale to call for banning flavored e-cigarettes. You know: *for the children*. But these men, like others espousing the ban, ignore two simple facts about e-cigarettes that should have them looking in different directions. First, e-cigarettes have not captured "a whole generation of young people." A cursory look at the data indicates that no more young people are vaping than smoked cigarettes in previous generations.[4] And second, e-cigarettes are often used as a smoking cessation product. One might expect a "smoking cessation expert" like Mr. Ylioja to be open to this possibility. One would be disappointed.

Busybullies are no less fervent in opposition to marijuana, which they seem to believe destroys lives, jobs, families, mothers, and even apple pie. They have pushed for ever more severe laws against its use over the years, and in their quest to "save" people from the evil weed, they empowered the government to destroy the lives, jobs, and families of anyone it found using the drug. Under their sway, government itself proved far more dangerous to marijuana users than marijuana ever was.

How do we know? Because as of 2019, ten states and the District of Columbia had legalized recreational marijuana, and thirty-three states plus D.C. had legalized medical marijuana—and yet all hell did not break loose.[5] In 2012, Colorado became the first state to legalize the buying and selling of recreational marijuana. Years later, busybullies in that state continue to argue for the government to reinstate prohibition. On the fifth anniversary of legalization, the *Colorado Springs Gazette* editorial board referred to what happened in Colorado as "an embarrassing cautionary tale" and gave a laundry list of supposed ill-effects of legalization, such as the smell of burning marijuana, increased homelessness, teen drug use, and an increase in fatal car accidents involving marijuana.[6] This last was puzzling, as no reliable DUI test for marijuana existed, and drug tests couldn't distinguish between marijuana ingested immediately before driving and marijuana ingested a month or more before driving.[7]

The editorial quoted Marijuana Accountability Coalition founder Justin Luke Riley playing the busybully's trump card: Riley claimed that legal marijuana was "devastating our kids and devastating whole communities." When all else fails, the busybullies plead that we think of the children. But they were not thinking about the children when the government was locking up parents on drug charges.

The data give the lie to the busybullies' overheated charges. The National Survey on Drug Use and Health revealed that in

2016 (the latest year for which data were available), little more than 9 percent of Colorado teenagers reported using marijuana.[8] Although that rate was higher than the national average for teenagers, it was the lowest Colorado had seen since 2007–8.[9] Meanwhile, alcohol, tobacco, and heroin use among Colorado teens all went down as well.

Then, in July 2019, the medical journal *JAMA Pediatrics* published the results of a comprehensive study of the effects of marijuana laws on teen marijuana use. Contrary to what the busybullies claimed, legalization simply had not increased teen drug use, the study determined. The lead researcher stated, "Just to be clear, we found no effect on teen use following legalization for medical purposes," and in fact the study found "evidence of a possible reduction in use following legalization for recreational purposes."[10]

It makes perfect sense that legalizing marijuana would not increase teen use. Legal cannabis business owners have strong incentives to check IDs. The prospect of going to jail is not the only thing that deters selling to minors. Owners of legal cannabis dispensaries must invest thousands of dollars in licensing fees and tens of thousands more in their physical shops.[11] A business owner who sells to minors stands to lose that investment. But under prohibition, the corner dealer, not having an investment at risk and facing the prospect of jail time with every sale, does not worry about selling to minors any more than he does about selling to adults.

Although marijuana legalization did not lead to the catastrophes busybullies had predicted, the Trump administration threatened to crack down on states that legalized marijuana.[12] Why? The White House and the Justice Department offered no actual reason, just the assertion that marijuana leads to opioid abuse.[13] Never mind that no studies have conclusively demonstrated this link.[14] And never mind that marijuana isn't an opioid in the first place. Facts don't matter when you have moral certainty.

President Trump's first Attorney General, Jeff Sessions, was the lead busybully on this issue. Sessions said that "good people don't smoke marijuana."[15] He called for the death penalty for marijuana dealers.[16] He asked Congress to let his Justice Department prosecute medical-marijuana providers.[17] He even claimed that marijuana is only "slightly less awful" than heroin.[18]

Perhaps not surprisingly, the Trump administration backed away from its hard-line stance on marijuana as Attorney General Sessions fell out of favor with the President. As the *Los Angeles Times* reported, in April 2018 President Trump "personally directed" the Justice Department to abandon its "threat to crack down on recreational marijuana in states where it is legal."[19] The busybullies finally backed off on this, but only after a clear majority of the states, with a clear corresponding percentage of the electorate, made it clear that this was the only workable choice.

So if legalization does not lead more minors to use marijuana, what effect does it have on crime? In early 2019, one prominent opponent of legalizing marijuana claimed that the first states to legalize saw "sharp increases in murders and aggravated assaults since 2014."[20] But a number of studies cast serious doubt on this claim. In fact, the most comprehensive study of the issue, released in October 2019, found "no statistically significant long-term effects of recreational cannabis laws or the initiation of retail sales on violent or property crime rates." The researchers concluded, "Marijuana legalization and sales have had minimal to no effect on major crimes."[21]

An earlier analysis comparing the three years in Colorado prior to legalization to the three years after legalization showed that Colorado's homicide, robbery, and burglary rates all went down after legalization.[22] But over the same period, they also went down for the country as a whole.[23] Relative to the United States, Colorado's homicide rate went down, but its robbery and burglary rates rose. In short the findings yielded a mixed bag. Based on only a few years' worth of data, they left the effect of marijuana legalization on all varieties of crime an open question.

Busybullies have complained that legalization led to increased homelessness. But the data tell a different story. From marijuana legalization in 2014 until 2018, homelessness in Denver dropped almost 14 percent.[24] In 2019, Denver's homelessness rate increased sharply, but it was still less than just prior to legalization.

Busybullies are quick to identify all sorts of evils that will befall society in the wake of marijuana legalization. But they are blind to the myriad evils that befall society because of prohibition. Today, more than a half million Americans are arrested each year for marijuana possession.[25] That's more than are arrested annually for all violent crimes combined.[26] Each one of those half million annual arrests represents a family that is subjected to significant financial, psychic, and sometimes physical harm from police, prosecutors, and courts.

Evidence from Colorado and other states shows that marijuana legalization does not lead to increased teen usage, does not necessarily lead to increased homelessness, and does not lead to societal breakdown. To the extent that marijuana does destroy lives, it is because busybullies demand that government destroy the lives of people who consume it.

## Taking Away Options

Bullying doesn't stop at marijuana. Busybullies across the country are working to declare pornography a "public health crisis." By 2019, sixteen state legislatures had passed official resolutions saying just that. In Utah and Virginia, busybullies said that pornography makes people less likely to get married, and in South Dakota, they pronounced that pornography leads to eating disorders.[27] Even if it is true that watching pornography makes a person less likely to marry, that's none of anyone else's business. Busybullies fight against pornography and, similarly,

> **If busybullies can decide everything, then we are no longer a nation of free and equal people**

prostitution because these offend their moral sensitivities. Absolutely, people need better options than selling their bodies, whether in person, in print, or online. But busybullies aren't interested in providing better options; they're interested in taking away what, for desperate people, might be some of the few remaining options they have. Thanks to the busybullies, sex workers don't have to choose between living on the streets and selling their bodies. They get to choose between living on the streets and going to jail.

It doesn't stop at porn and prostitution, either. Busybullies tried to force Philadelphians to make healthier choices by supporting a tax on sugary drinks.[28] The tax went into effect, nearly doubling soda prices. The result? People wanting a sugar fix simply bought untaxed soda outside the city limits.[29] Meanwhile, inside the city, soda sales plummeted, and people working for beverage distributors, grocery stores, and convenience stores lost their jobs.[30]

One sad consequence of all this bullying is a deteriorating relationship between police and their communities.[31] To impose their wills on others, busybullies co-opt the power of government, power that ultimately manifests in the police. Every regulation, no matter how apparently benign, comes with the implied threat of violence. And the police are the instrument of that violence. Try to sell cigarettes without paying the appropriate taxes, and you will be fined. Refuse to pay the fine, and you will receive a summons. Ignore the summons, and the police will show up to take you to court. Resist, and the police will use force to subdue you. For an example, see Eric Garner, whom New York City police killed during an altercation about whether he had paid taxes on the cigarettes he was selling.[32]

Each regulation that busybullies promulgate diverts law enforcement resources from stopping criminals to stopping people from doing things of which the busybullies disapprove. Understandably, people start to mistrust and resent the police. In turn, the police become wary of the people. The people see this wariness and become even more distrustful. This antagonistic cycle begins with an understandable lack of respect for laws that are nothing more than codified nosiness.

Our ancestors sought freedom to escape tyranny to the extent possible. Yet today we are less free because some among us believe they know better what is good for us than we do for ourselves. Whether they are correct is irrelevant. If busybullies can decide what we should and should not put in our bodies, where we should and should not spend our money, and how we should and should not earn our livings, then we are no longer a nation of free and equal people. We aren't even a nation of children—for children eventually grow up. We are a nation of pets, to be guided, cared for, and reprimanded by our betters.

The shame of the whole ordeal is that busybullies are taken seriously at all, because they really strive to regulate people's behavior so that it mirrors their own. This is antithetical to a free society. When government becomes a hammer with which some beat others into submission, coercion replaces cooperation. When some get to wield that hammer over others, inequality replaces equality.

When it comes to promoting cooperation and preserving equality, the opening phrase "Government should…" is dangerous, though on occasion it's necessary for promoting the general welfare. But when "Government should..." is followed by "...because I don't like...," government has become a tool for elevating some people's preferences over others'. The automatic response should be "Too bad."

# 10

# COOPERATION

Humans live a dual existence. We are individuals with individual desires, knowledge, and abilities, but we are also members of communities and have connections and interactions with others. This tension between the human-as-individual and the human-as-member-of-society raises the question of when it is best for people to make decisions for themselves and when it is best for decisions to be made for them. That is, when is it appropriate to regard a person first as an individual who has the right to do as he will versus first as a member of society who has obligations to society's other members?

Societies address this question of our dual existence differently, relying sometimes on spontaneous order (cooperation that arises from individual action) and sometimes on central planning (coercion that arises from collective action). Evidence and reason suggest that neither approach, alone, is adequate. In a society in which there is only individual action, the physically and financially strong will harm the weak. But in a society in which there is only collective action, the politically strong will harm the weak.

In previous chapters, we have seen examples in which the collective action of central planning is too difficult to achieve, too expensive to maintain, prone to undesirable outcomes, or all of the above. For these reasons, the individual action of spontaneous order tends to yield superior results.

Yet if spontaneous order is superior, why do governments arise? Never has a society of humans evolved in which the individuals have not come together to construct a government. Some of those governments have been quite rudimentary, some have remained limited, and some have grown to become deeply coercive. But history has repeatedly demonstrated that governments do arise. And where governments are needed but don't exist, free people create a sort of government in their place. Neighbors form homeowners associations and contractually agree to live by their covenants. People agree to have neutral arbitrators decide their disputes and agree to abide by the arbitrators' rulings. Private universities form private police forces to maintain order and security. Entrepreneurs develop rating agencies that monitor products and inform consumers about product safety.

If too much government permits coercion by the politically strong, and too little government permits coercion by the physically and financially strong, how much government is best?

To answer that question, we can look at examples of societies that have relied more on coercion and ones that have relied more on cooperation. No perfect measure exists to gauge societies on a scale from too little government to too much government. But we know we need a reality-based measure that gets beyond people's stated intentions. Stalin's Soviet Union presented itself as a society that valued the individual. In reality, it did no such thing.

The best reality-based measure is probably economic freedom. Economic freedom measures the extent to which a society's people are free to make decisions for themselves while simultaneously being prevented from harming others. This is what Thomas Jefferson had in mind during his First Inaugural Address when he said that "wise" government "shall restrain men from injuring one another" but "shall leave them otherwise free to regulate their own pursuits."[1] In practice, more economic freedom is consonant with societies that rely more on cooperation, while less economic freedom is consonant with societies that rely more on coercion.

Once we have determined the level of economic freedom in various societies, we can see how well or poorly those societies have functioned. Societies that function well will be more affluent than societies that do not. They will also experience less unemployment, less poverty, less exploitation, and less income inequality than do societies that do not function well.

> "A wise and frugal Government, which shall restrain men from injuring one another, shall leave them otherwise free to regulate their own pursuits"
>
> —Thomas Jefferson

## Cooperation and Coercion Among the Fifty States

Several organizations attempt to measure economic freedom. Here we use the measure from the Fraser Institute. Fraser's data set is the broadest, encompassing cities, states, and countries, over almost four decades.[2]

Let's begin by looking at the United States. We can divide the fifty states into two groups according to the degree of economic freedom in each. The twenty-five states that fall above the median for economic freedom we'll call the "more cooperative states." The twenty-five states that fall below the median for economic freedom we'll call the "more coercive states."

Keep in mind that when we talk about "cooperative" and "coercive" states, we are talking about *relative* differences among states. After all, Americans, no matter what state they live in, enjoy high levels of economic freedom overall.

It is also important to note that economic freedom does not mean "less government"; it means "right government." A society whose government, through inaction, fails to protect people's property rights is as economically unfree as a society whose government actively violates people's property rights.

Over time, individual states will not necessarily remain in the same categories. For the period 1981 through 2015, thirteen

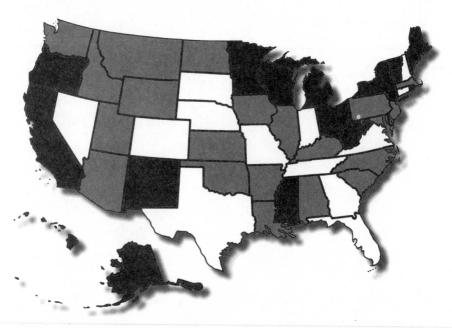

*Data source: Fraser Institute. Over the period 1981 through 2015, states in black appear in the more coercive category in every year. States in white appear in the more cooperative category in every year. States in gray move between the groups at least once.*

states appeared in the more cooperative category in every year, fifteen states appeared in the more coercive category every year, and the remaining twenty-two states moved back and forth between the two groups. At the low end, Arkansas, Maryland, South Carolina, and Washington switched groups once each. At the high end, Idaho, Kansas, and Kentucky switched back and forth eight times.

We can cross-reference the data on economic freedom with median household income (adjusted for inflation). In 1984, the earliest year for which data were readily available at the state level, the median household income for the twenty-five more coopera-tive states averaged more than $49,700 (in 2016 dollars).[3] That same year, the median household income for the twenty-five more coercive states averaged just over $49,600. The next year, 1985, median household income was again higher (on average) for the twenty-five more cooperative states than for the twenty-five more coercive states—more than $50,000 versus $48,700.

In fact, when we perform the comparison for each year from 1984 through 2014, we find that the twenty-five more cooperative

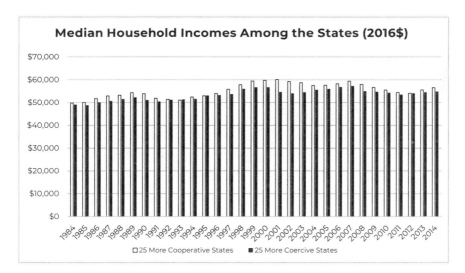

*Data sources: Census Bureau and Fraser Institute*

states had higher median household incomes in all but two years (1993 and 1995). Almost 95 percent of the time, then, people in more cooperative states were more affluent than were people in more coercive states.

A similar pattern emerges with poverty rates.[4] In twenty-nine out of thirty-four years, or more than 85 percent of the time, the twenty-five more cooperative states experienced lower poverty rates (on average) than did the twenty-five more coercive states.

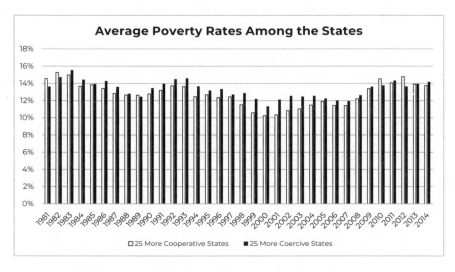

*Data sources: Census Bureau, Bureau of Economic Analysis, and Fraser Institute*

Remember that the two groups are not the same states from one year to the next. Almost half of the fifty states moved back and forth between the two groups over the years. This makes it less likely that what we are seeing results from some other factor—such as climate, access to waterways, population, or history—that might, coincidentally, be correlated with cooperation and coercion.

When we cross-reference economic freedom with unemployment, the same pattern emerges.[5] From 1981 through 2014, in all but two years (1998 and 2010), the twenty-five more cooperative states exhibited lower average unemployment rates than did the twenty-five more coercive states.

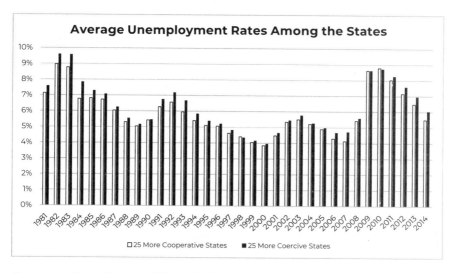

*Data sources: Census Bureau and Fraser Institute*

## Cooperation and Coercion Among Countries

Among countries, there are natural economic experiments that illustrate the different effects of cooperation and coercion.

North and South Korea are two countries populated by the same ethnic people, sharing the same climate, and with access to the same natural resources and similar waterways. Prior to 1950, they even shared the same history. But beginning in 1950, the two countries diverged. North Korea's government came to rely heavily on coercion, while South Korea's relied largely on cooperation. Today, North Korea ranks last in the world for economic freedom, whereas South Korea ranks thirty-third out of 151 countries. South Korea's per capita income is now somewhere between fourteen and forty times that of North Korea.[6]

The difference in standards of living has caused differences in food intake that have left the average adult North Korean one to three inches shorter than the average adult South Korean.[7] South Korea's poverty rate is below 15 percent.[8] North Korea's poverty rate is unknown, but reports from people who have fled the country suggest that as much as 50 percent of the North Korean population could live in extreme poverty.[9]

The island of Hispaniola is divided almost down the middle, with Haiti on the west side and the Dominican Republic on the east. Even before the 2010 earthquake that devastated Haiti's economy, average income in the Dominican Republic (sixty-sixth most economically free) was more than nine times that in Haiti (ninety-second most economically free). Prior to the earthquake, the poverty rate in the Dominican Republic was a whopping 42 percent, yet it was far lower than Haiti's 60 percent.

These cases are just individual examples, but if we look at all the countries of the world, we see the same trend that we

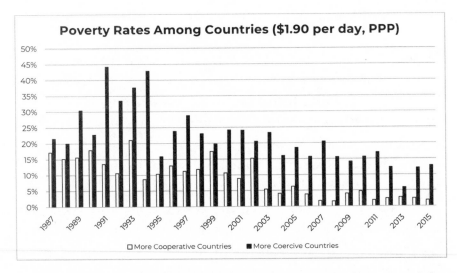

*Data sources: World Bank and Fraser Institute. The poverty rates are in "purchase power parity" terms and so account for differences in the costs of living across countries.*

saw in the fifty states. Using economic freedom measures for countries, we can similarly divide the countries of the world into those that rely more on cooperation and those that rely more on coercion. If we look at extreme poverty rates among reporting countries, we see that the more cooperative countries exhibited lower poverty rates (on average) than did the more coercive countries.[10]

Of course, it could be that we are simply seeing that people in rich countries both experience less poverty and have the leisure and ability to secure economic freedom. Put another way, is cooperation simply a coincidental by-product of being rich?

One way to address this question is to look at the poor countries only.[11] Here again the familiar pattern emerges. Poor countries that relied more on cooperation experienced less poverty than did poor countries that relied more on coercion.[12]

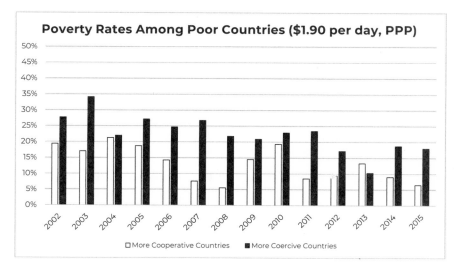

*Data sources: World Bank and Fraser Institute. The poverty rates are in "purchase power parity" terms and so account for differences in the costs of living across countries.*

The poverty definition of $1.90 per day is the World Bank's most extreme poverty measure.[13] If we use the more relaxed measure of $5.50 per day, we get the same results both when comparing countries in general and when comparing poor countries.

As one might expect at this point, average incomes (as measured by per capita GDP) were higher among the more cooperative countries. The pattern also holds among the poor countries. In every year except 1976, poor countries that relied more on cooperation exhibited higher incomes than did poor countries that relied more on coercion.[14]

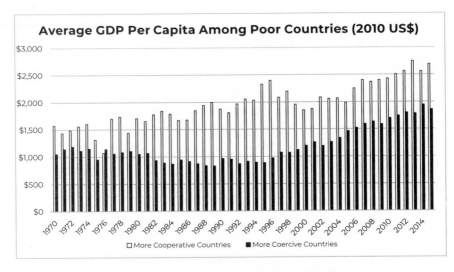

*Data sources: World Bank and Fraser Institute. Data are adjusted for inflation.*

Perhaps more cooperation yields better average incomes, but only at the cost of more pronounced inequality. Further, since coercion is necessary for income redistribution, one might expect the more cooperative countries to exhibit more income inequality.

We can explore this issue by looking at the Gini Index, a measure of inequality that ranges from 0 (perfect equality) to 100 (perfect inequality). The World Bank maintains a database of Gini estimates from a variety of sources, and here we take the average of these estimates.[15] For more than two-thirds of the years from 1983 through 2010, more cooperative countries exhibited less inequality than did more coercive countries. Interestingly, the same pattern emerges when we compare the fifty U.S. states: those that were more economically free exhibited less income inequality than did those that were less economically free.

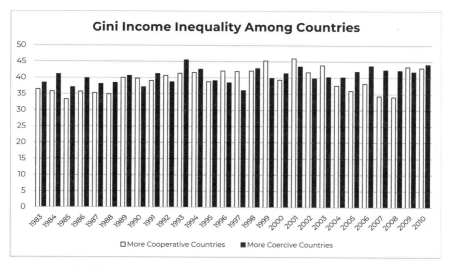

*Data sources: World Bank and Fraser Institute*

Financial figures do not constitute the only measures of a well-functioning society. We should look, for example, at the quality of life for marginalized people. Throughout history, different groups have been marginalized at different times. But across countries, cultures, and time, two demographic groups tend to appear often among those treated with less dignity: women and children.

The United Nations Development Programme (UNDP) measures gender equality across countries. Its measure attempts to capture the quality of life (with respect to income, education, and health) of women versus men. In a country with greater gender inequality, women have a lower quality of life than do men in that country. The UNDP reported gender inequality for

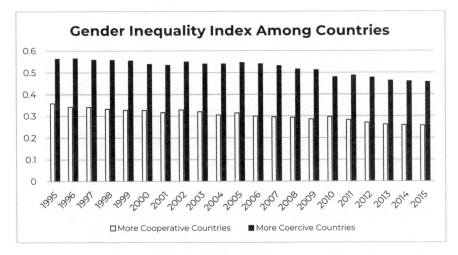

*Data sources: United Nations Development Programme and Fraser Institute. The UNDP reports the Gender Inequality Index only for the years 1995, 2000, 2005, and 2010 through 2015. The inequality indices for the intervening years are interpolated.*

between 101 and 144 countries over the period 1995 through 2015.[16] In every year, the more cooperative countries exhibited less gender inequality than did the more coercive countries.

Again, though, we need to ask: do countries tend to perform better on this metric not because they are more cooperative but simply because they are richer? And once more, the way to answer this question is to examine only the poorer countries.

When we do so, we find the same result.[17] Women in poor countries that relied more on cooperation suffered less gender inequality than did women in poor countries that relied more on coercion.

Child labor rates also show this pattern. We would expect child labor rates to be lower for more cooperative countries (and they are) because more cooperative countries are also more affluent. But we might expect to see the reverse among poor countries. That's because poor countries that rely less on the coercive force of government to regulate labor markets could have lax child labor laws. Unscrupulous employers from rich countries

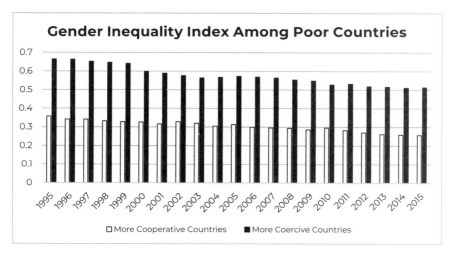

Data sources: *United Nations Development Programme and Fraser Institute*

might take advantage by moving manufacturing operations to those less regulated countries.

That, however, is not the case. Among the approximately fifty reporting poor countries, child labor rates were lower among

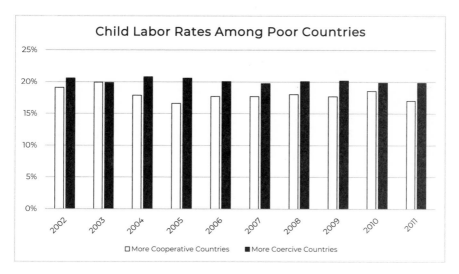

Data sources: *United Nations Children's Fund and Fraser Institute*

the more cooperative countries than among the more coercive countries.[18] It seems that, with the greater individual choice that comes in a society relying more on cooperation, parents are more able to find alternatives to having their children work.

The results we see here persist if we compare cooperation and coercion among cities within the United States.[19] The data tell a remarkably consistent story. Across cities, states, countries, and time, societies that rely more on cooperation exhibit the hallmarks we associate with healthier societies.

Across cities, states, countries, and time, societies that rely more on cooperation exhibit the hallmarks of healthier societies

Both reason and the data we've seen here suggest a rule for good governance. A good government is one that allows people to do as they will provided they don't harm one another. This is what Thomas Jefferson was trying to tell us more than two centuries ago.

## The Appropriate Size of Government

People of goodwill who seek more expansive government and people of goodwill who seek more limited government have the same goal: they want to make life better for people. They agree on ends; they simply disagree on means. Their primary source of disagreement is in how much faith they place in government's ability to help meet their shared goal. Those who seek more expansive government see government as a tool for making people's lives better. Those who seek more limited government see government as an impediment.

The truth is somewhere in between. When government is too small and inconsequential, the rich and powerful can take advantage of government's weakness to make life better for themselves and worse for everyone else. But when government becomes too large and intrusive, the rich and powerful can take advantage of government's strength to do the same.

So when is government large enough but not too large? What is that optimal size?

Where the United States is concerned, we can turn again to evidence for a clue. For the past seventy years, regardless of whether the U.S. federal government has set tax rates high or set them low, regardless of whether it has taxed people or corporations or estates, regardless of whether it has taxed wages or investment income or imports, one thing has remained relatively constant: the federal government collects about 17 percent of the economy in tax revenue. It appears that, ignoring what size of government is best, Americans have arrived at a practical answer—that they prefer a federal government whose budget is about 17 percent of the economy. That's a somewhat smaller federal government than we have now. Over the same period that the federal government's revenues have averaged 17 percent of the economy, its spending has averaged 19 percent of the economy. And that figure rose to almost 22 percent in the decade between 2009 and 2018.[20]

Of course, the financial size of government is only one ingredient in establishing the right size of government. The other is determining what government does with its financial resources. A government that devotes its resources to establishing laws and regulations that prevent people from harming others spends its resources well. A government that devotes its resources to establishing laws and regulations that favor special interests does not.

What the financial data make clear, however, is that our government is clearly living beyond its means. This leads to all kinds of problems, and they are the most unfair kind: the kind we foist on future generations. Government debt is not the answer. We also need to stop wishing, hoping, and expecting that the government will magically be composed of the best and the brightest. The government will be no better and no worse than the general population.

More than this, we must acknowledge that evidence matters, because no quantity of good intentions will change the facts. Human beings can accomplish quite a lot, but none of us knows all that much individually. So expecting people in government to be able to make things as complicated as pencils, toasters, and sandwiches, let alone to address issues as complex as healthcare, education, and welfare for a nation of 330 million people, is the search for fool's gold.

Finally, we need to understand and admit that reasonable people disagree on what the good life entails, and the more effort we expend bullying one another with the power of government, the fewer of us will be living the good life.

Whatever else it is, the good life consists of massive amounts of human cooperation, and only as much coercion as is absolutely necessary. And that is as good a place to end as it is to begin.

# NOTES

## Introduction: Cooperation and Coercion

1 Drew DeSilver, "U.S. Trails Most Developed Countries in Voter Turnout," Pew Research Center, May 21, 2018, https://www.pewresearch.org/fact-tank/2018/05/21/u-s-voter-turnout-trails-most-developed-countries/ (accessed December 9, 2019).

2 Thomas Paine, *Common Sense* (1776), https://oll.libertyfund.org/pages/1776-paine-common-sense-pamphlet (accessed December 9, 2019).

## Chapter 1: The Knowledge Problem

1 Thomas Thwaites, "The Toaster Project," http://www.thomasthwaites.com/the-toaster-project/ (accessed August 28, 2019).

2 "Code of Federal Regulations Total Pages 1938–1949, and Total Volumes and Pages 1950–2017," Federal Register, https://www.federalregister.gov/uploads/2018/03/cfrTotalPages2017.pdf (accessed October 16, 2019).

3 Stephen J. Dubner, "The Cobra Effect: A New Freakonomics Radio Podcast," *Freakonomics*, October 11, 2012.

4 Michael G. Vann and Liz Clarke, *The Great Hanoi Rat Hunt: Empire, Disease, and Modernity in French Colonial Vietnam* (New York: Oxford University Press, 2018).

5 Sam Peltzman, "The Effects of Automobile Safety Regulation," *Journal of Political Economy* 83, no. 4 (August 1975), https://www.jstor.org/stable/1830396. Forty

years after the publication of Peltzman's article, economist Jim Leitzel noted that many subsequent studies had confirmed the findings: "The studies tend to replicate the finding of some countervailing effects following heightened safety regulation." Jim Leitzel, *Concepts in Law and Economics: A Guide for the Curious* (New York: Oxford University Press, 2015), 72.

6    Tamar Lapin, "Uber Driver Was Streaming Hulu Show Before Fatal Self-Driving Crash," *New York Post*, June 22, 2018, https://nypost.com/2018/06/22/uber-driver-was-streaming-hulu-show-before-fatal-self-driving-crash/.

7    Daron Acemoglu and Joshua Angrist, "Consequences of Employment Protection? The Case of the Americans with Disabilities Act," NBER Working Paper No. 6670, July 1998, https://www.nber.org/papers/w6670.pdf (accessed August 28, 2019).

8    Lucas W. Davis, "The Effect of Driving Restrictions on Air Quality in Mexico City," *Journal of Political Economy* 116, no. 1 (February 2008): 38–81, https://www.jstor.org/stable/10.1086/529398?seq=1#page_scan_tab_contents.

9    "Inflation Rate, End of Period Consumer Prices," IMF DataMapper, https://www.imf.org/external/datamapper/PCPIEPCH@WEO/VEN (accessed August 28, 2019). See also Steve Hanke, "Venezuela's Hyperinflation, 24 Months and Counting," *Forbes*, October 23, 2018, https://www.forbes.com/sites/stevehanke/2018/10/23/venezuelas-hyperinflation-24-months-and-counting/ (accessed August 28, 2019).

10   Robert Tracinski, "In Venezuela's Socialist Paradise, Workers Report to Labor Camps," *The Federalist*, August 1, 2016, http://thefederalist.com/2016/08/01/in-venezuelas-socialist-paradise-workers-report-to-labor-camps/ (accessed August 28, 2019).

11   Friedrich A. von Hayek, *The Fatal Conceit: The Errors of Socialism* (Chicago: University of Chicago Press, 1988), 76.

12   "Nicaraguan Sign Language," Ethnologue: Languages of the World, https://www.ethnologue.com/18/language/ncs/ (accessed October 16, 2019).

13   "Key Facts about the Uninsured Population," Henry J. Kaiser Family Foundation, December 7, 2018, https://www.kff.org/uninsured/fact-sheet/key-facts-about-the-uninsured-population/ (accessed August 28, 2019).


## Chapter 2: Rights and Wrongs

1    "Homer vs. the Eighteenth Amendment," *The Simpsons*, season 8, episode 18.

2    Thomas Jefferson, letter to Roger C. Weightman, June 24, 1826.


## Chapter 3: The Magic Wand

1    President Franklin D. Roosevelt, State of the Union Message to Congress, January 11, 1944, http://www.fdrlibrary.marist.edu/archives/address_text.html (accessed August 30, 2019).

2    You can imagine greater complexity wherein voters in group B face a "free-rider" problem. If you are in group B and you know that the law is likely to pass, you have an incentive not to vote. That way, you gain $45 from the law passing without incurring the $20 voting cost. But notice that the free-rider problem also exists for group A. As a member of group A, you suspect that, because of the free-rider prob-

lem in group B, most of the group B voters will choose not to vote. So you know that the law stands a good chance of being defeated if only some group A voters step up to vote. But you have an incentive not to vote so as to save the $20 voting fee while leaving the voting to other group A voters.

3   Brenna Goth, "Construction, Transit Groups Fund Phoenix Prop. 104 Transit Tax Campaign," *Arizona Republic*, July 1, 2015, http://www.azcentral.com/story/news/local/phoenix/2015/07/01/construction-transit-groups-fund-transit-tax-campaign/29575221/ (accessed August 30, 2019); "Important Change: New 2020 Threshold Amounts for the Retail Sales and Use Tax Two-Level Tax Rate Structure Under the Comprehensive Transportation Plan Effective January 1, 2020," City of Phoenix Finance Department, Tax Division, https://www.phoenix.gov/financesite/Documents/Taxpayer%20Bulletin%20to%20Filers%202020.pdf (accessed December 2, 2019).

4   Voter Registration Counts, State of Arizona, https://azsos.gov/elections/voter-registration-historical-election-data/voter-registration-counts (accessed August 30, 2019).

5   Brenna Goth, "Phoenix Voters Pass Prop. 104 Transit Tax," *Arizona Republic*, August 25, 2015, http://www.azcentral.com/story/news/local/phoenix/2015/08/25/phoenix-elections-transit-results-prop104/32283455/ (accessed August 30, 2019).

6   Thomas Sowell, "Solving Whose Problem?" *Townhall*, November 24, 2009, https://townhall.com/columnists/thomassowell/2009/11/24/solving-whose-problem-n895737 (accessed December 11, 2019).

7   Dennis Wagner, "Phoenix VA Officials Knew of False Data for 2 Years," *Arizona Republic*, June 21, 2014, https://www.azcentral.com/story/news/arizona/investigations/2014/06/22/phoenix-va-officials-false-data/11232447/ (accessed August 30, 2019).

8   Donovan Slack and Dennis Wagner, "6 Big Things the New Veterans Affairs Chief Will Have to Address," *USA Today*, March 29, 2018, https://www.usatoday.com/story/news/politics/2018/03/29/veterans-affairs-failures-go-beyond-ousted-secout-live-three-secretaries-soon-four-including-david-sh/470573002/ (accessed December 10, 2019).

9   Hope Yen, "U.S. Postal Service Marks 11 Straight Years of Financial Loss," Associated Press, November 14, 2017, https://www.pbs.org/newshour/nation/u-s-postal-service-marks-11-straight-years-of-financial-loss (accessed August 30, 2019).

## Chapter 4: The Minimum Wage

1   President Barack Obama, State of the Union Address, February 12, 2013, http://www.whitehouse.gov/the-press-office/2013/02/12/remarks-president-state-union-address (accessed September 17, 2019).

2   Niv Elis, "Poll: Bipartisan Majority Supports Raising Minimum Wage," *The Hill*, June 1, 2017, https://thehill.com/homenews/335837-poll-bipartisan-majority-supports-raising-minimum-wage (accessed September 17, 2019).

3   "Computer and Internet Access in the United States: 2012," U.S. Census Bureau, https://www.census.gov/data/tables/2012/demo/computer-internet/computer-use-2012.html (accessed September 17, 2019).

4   For more details, see "Korean Grocer Learns the Law Doesn't Care About His Good Deeds," *Wall Street Journal*, July 30, 1996.

5    The story is complicated by the fact that the Mathews brothers were eleven and twelve years old. The Department of Labor said that they fined Choi both because he wasn't paying the brothers the minimum wage and because the brothers were too young to work legally. The effect of the government's declaring someone too young to work is, from an economic perspective, identical to the effect of a minimum wage. Banning someone from working is identical to imposing an infinite minimum wage—that is, there is no wage at which the person can legally work. See Maria Echaveste, Letter to the Editor, *Wall Street Journal*, September 6, 1996, https://www.wsj.com/articles/SB841966791776547500 (accessed September 18, 2019).

6    "Fact Sheet #71: Internship Programs Under the Fair Labor Standards Act," U.S. Department of Labor, January 2018, http://www.dol.gov/whd/regs/compliance/ whdfs71.htm (accessed September 17, 2019).

7    Stephen Lurie, "How the Senate Exploits Unpaid Interns," *The Atlantic*, August 29, 2013, http://www.theatlantic.com/politics/archive/2013/08/how-the-senate- exploits-unpaid-interns/279111/ (accessed September 17, 2019).

8    William J. Carrington and Bruce C. Fallick, "Do Some Workers Have Minimum Wage Careers?" *Monthly Labor Review*, May 2001, http://www.bls.gov/opub/ mlr/2001/05/art2full.pdf (accessed September 17, 2019).

9    "Characteristics of Minimum Wage Workers, 2017," Bureau of Labor Statistics, https://www.bls.gov/opub/reports/minimum-wage/2017/home.htm (accessed September 17, 2019; "All Employees, Total Nonfarm," Federal Reserve Bank of St. Louis, December 6, 2019, https://fred.stlouisfed.org/series/PAYEMS#0 (accessed December 11, 2019).

10    Ibid.

11    Ibid.

12    Ibid.

13    Ibid.

14    James Sherk, "Who Earns the Minimum Wage? Suburban Teenagers, Not Single Parents," Heritage Foundation, February 28, 2013, http://www.heritage.org/ research/reports/2013/02/who-earns-the-minimum-wage-suburban-teenagers-not-single-parents (accessed September 17, 2019).

15    "Employed Full Time: Median Usual Weekly Nominal Earnings (Second Quartile): Wage and Salary Workers: 16 Years and Over," Federal Reserve Bank of St. Louis, July 17, 2019, https://fred.stlouisfed.org/series/LES1252881500Q (accessed September 17, 2019).

16    Antony Davies, "Unintended Consequences of Raising the Minimum Wage," Mercatus Center at George Mason University, October 25, 2013, http://mercatus.org/ sites/default/files/unintended-consequences-raising-minimum-wage.pdf (accessed September 17, 2019).

17    "Table A-4: Employment Status of the Civilian Population 25 Years and Over by Educational Attainment," Bureau of Labor Statistics, http://www.bls.gov/ webapps/legacy/cpsatab4.htm; U.S. Census Bureau, "Labor Force, Employment, and Earnings," *Statistical Abstract of the United States*, October 1996, https://www2. census.gov/library/publications/1996/compendia/statab/116ed/tables/labor.pdf; "Federal Minimum Hourly Wage for Nonfarm Workers for the United States," Federal Reserve Bank of St. Louis, August 30, 2019, https://fred.stlouisfed.org/ series/FEDMINNFRWG; "National Average Wage Indexing Series, 1951–2017,"

Social Security Administration, https://www.ssa.gov/oact/cola/AWI.html#Series (all links accessed September 17, 2019).

18  Press Release, "House GOP Votes Against Considering Call Center Bill, Aligns Itself Against U.S. Workers and Consumers," Communications Workers of America, June 19, 2012, http://www.cwa-union.org/news/entry/house_gop_votes_against_considering_call_center_bill_aligns_itself_against_#.UCqPbjFYvp8 (accessed September 17, 2019).

19  Richard Berman, "Why Unions Want a Higher Minimum Wage," *Wall Street Journal*, February 25, 2013, https://www.wsj.com/articles/SB1000142412788732404890457 8318541000422454 (accessed September 17, 2019).

20  James Sherk, "Union Members, Not Minimum-Wage Earners, Benefit When the Minimum Wage Rises," Heritage Foundation, February 7, 2007, https://www.heritage.org/jobs-and-labor/report/union-members-not-minimum-wage-earners-benefit-when-the-minimumwage-rises (accessed September 17, 2019).

21  "Labor," OpenSecrets.org, Center for Responsive Politics, https://www.opensecrets.org/industries/indus.php?ind=P (accessed October 1, 2019).

## Chapter 5: Gun Control

1  *Special Report of the Paris Anti-Slavery Conference, Held on the 26th and 27th August, 1867* (London: Committee of the British and Foreign Anti-Slavery Society, 1867), https://babel.hathitrust.org/cgi/pt?id=nyp.33433081995270;view=1up;seq=11 (accessed September 19, 2019).

2  The ATF existed prior to 1972 as part of larger agencies.

3  "President Obama's Remarks on New Gun Control Actions, Jan. 16, 2013 (Transcript)," *Washington Post*, January 16, 2013, https://www.washingtonpost.com/politics/president-obamas-remarks-on-new-gun-control-proposals-jan-16-2013-transcript/2013/01/16/528e7758-5ffc-11e2-b05a-605528f6b712_story.html (accessed December 9, 2019); Charles C. W. Cooke, " 'If It Saves One Life . . . ,' " *National Review Online*, January 9, 2013, https://www.nationalreview.com/corner/if-it-saves-one-life-charles-c-w-cooke/ (accessed December 9, 2019).

4  "15th Person Dies After Truck Crash in Texas," Associated Press, July 24, 2012, https://www.cbsnews.com/news/15th-person-dies-after-truck-crash-in-texas/ (accessed September 19, 2019).

5  Erica Ritz, "Massacre Survivor Tells Senate: I'm Not a Victim of Guns, but of Lawmakers Who 'Legislated Me Out of the Right to Protect Myself and My Family," *The Blaze*, February 14, 2013, https://www.theblaze.com/news/2013/02/14/famous-luby-massacre-survivor-to-senate-im-not-a-victim-of-guns-but-of-lawmakers-who-legislated-me-out-of-the-right-to-protect-myself-and-my-family (accessed September 19, 2019).

6  Donna L. Hoyert and Jiaquan Xu, "Deaths: Preliminary Data for 2011," *National Vital Statistics Reports* 61, no. 6, http://www.cdc.gov/nchs/data/nvsr/nvsr61/nvsr61_06.pdf (accessed September 19, 2019).

7  "For Sandy Hook Killer's Father, Tragedy Outweighs Love for His Son," *Fresh Air*, NPR, March 13, 2014, http://www.npr.org/2014/03/13/289815818/6-interviews-1-reckoning-sandy-hook-killers-dad-breaks-silence (accessed September 19, 2019).

8    Rick Ungar, "Here Are the 23 Executive Orders on Gun Safety Signed Today by the President," *Forbes*, January 16, 2013, http://www.forbes.com/sites/rickungar/2013/01/16/here-are-the-23-executive-orders-on-gun-safety-signed-today-by-the-president/ (accessed September 19, 2019).

9    Alan I. Leshner et al., eds., *Priorities for Research to Reduce the Threat of Firearm-Related Violence* (Washington, DC: National Academies Press, 2013), https://www.nap.edu/read/18319/chapter/1 (accessed September 19, 2019).

10   Mark Follman, Gavin Aronsen, and Deanna Pan, "U.S. Mass Shootings, 1982–2019: Data from *Mother Jones*' Investigation," *Mother Jones*, August 31, 2019, http://www.motherjones.com/politics/2012/12/mass-shootings-mother-jones-full-data (accessed October 1, 2019).

11   "Table 4: Crime in the United States," FBI, https://ucr.fbi.gov/crime-in-the-u.s/2018/crime-in-the-u.s.-2018/topic-pages/tables/table-4 (accessed October 1, 2019).

12   "Fatal Injury Reports, National and Regional, 1999–2015," Centers for Disease Control and Prevention, June 24, 2015, http://webappa.cdc.gov/sasweb/ncipc/mortrate10_us.html (accessed September 19, 2019).

13   Leshner et al., *Priorities for Research to Reduce the Threat of Firearm-Related Violence.*

14   Rich Phillips, "Gun Rights Groups Say Georgia Home Invasion Proves Their Point," CNN, January 11, 2013, http://www.cnn.com/2013/01/10/us/home-invasion-gun-rights/index.html (accessed September 19, 2019).

15   "Guns," Gallup, https://www.gallup.com/poll/1645/guns.aspx (accessed September 19, 2019).

16   FBI, "Murder Rate, 1960–2014," Uniform Crime Reporting Statistics, https://www.bjs.gov/ucrdata/Search/Crime/State/RunCrimeTrendsInOneVar.cfm (accessed September 19, 2019).

17   "Guns," Gallup; FBI, "Murder Rate, 1960–2014." Due to sporadic polling in the early years, the following years are interpolated: 1960–64, 1966, 1967, 1969–71, 1973, 1974, 1976–79, 1981, 1982, 1984, 1986–88, 1992, 1994, 1995, 1998.

18   "Guns," Gallup; Follman, Aronsen, and Pan, "U.S. Mass Shootings, 1982–2019: Data from *Mother Jones*' Investigation." We show the fatality rate, not the casualty rate, because the 2017 Las Vegas shooting had 546 injuries, more than seven times the average. That single data point overwhelms the casualty chart. Excluding the Las Vegas incident, the graph for casualties has the same general shape as the graph for fatalities shown here.

19   Annual Survey Data, Behavioral Risk Factor Surveillance System, Centers for Disease Control and Prevention, http://www.cdc.gov/brfss/annual_data/annual_data.htm; "Fatal Injury Reports, National, Regional, and State, 1981–2017," Centers for Disease Control and Prevention, http://www.cdc.gov/injury/wisqars/fatal_injury_reports.html (accessed September 19, 2019).

20   Annual Survey Data, Behavioral Risk Factor Surveillance System; "Fatal Injury Reports, National, Regional, and State, 1981–2017." No bar indicates that the state did not report data.

21   "Fatal Injury Reports, National, Regional, and State, 1981–2017."

22   Annual Survey Data, Behavioral Risk Factor Surveillance System; "Fatal Injury Reports, National, Regional, and State, 1981–2017." No bar indicates that the state did not report data.

23   "Violence-Related Firearm Deaths Among Residents of Metropolitan Areas and Cities—United States, 2006–2007," *Morbidity and Mortality Weekly Report*, May 13,

2011, http://www.cdc.gov/mmwr/pdf/wk/mm6018.pdf (accessed September 19, 2019).

24 Mona Chalabi, "Gun Homicides and Gun Ownership Listed by Country," *Guardian*, July 22, 2012, http://www.guardian.co.uk/news/datablog/2012/jul/22/gun-homicides-ownership-world-list; United Nations Office on Drugs and Crime, https://docs.google.com/spreadsheets/d/1chqUZHuY6cXYrRYkuE0uwXisGaYvr7durZHJhpLGycs/edit#gid=0 (accessed September 19, 2019). The vertical axis is on a logarithmic scale so as to make the shorter bars visible. The logarithmic scale has the effect of diminishing the difference in heights between the taller and shorter bars, but this does not detract from the purpose of the graph. The purpose is to demonstrate that, as you move from left (higher gun-ownership rates) to right (lower gun-ownership rates), the heights of the bars do not decline.

25 "Trends in Homicide, 1989–90 to 2013–14," Crime Statistics Australia, Australian Institute of Criminology, http://crimestats.aic.gov.au/NHMP/1_trends/ (accessed September 19, 2019).

26 "Trends in Homicide, 1989–90 to 2013–14"; "Fatal Injury Reports, National, Regional, and State, 1981–2017"; "United States Crime Rates 1960–2018," DisasterCenter.com, http://www.disastercenter.com/crime/uscrime.htm (accessed October 8, 2019).

27 Michael Planty and Jennifer L. Truman, "Firearm Violence, 1993–2011," Bureau of Justice Statistics, May 2013, http://www.bjs.gov/content/pub/pdf/fv9311.pdf (accessed September 19, 2019).

28 Ibid.

## Chapter 6: Wars on Nouns

1 Stephen Daggett, "Costs of Major U.S. Wars," Congressional Research Service, June 29, 2010, https://fas.org/sgp/crs/natsec/RS22926.pdf (accessed October 3, 2019).

2 Ibid.

3 "Roosevelt Signs Executive Order 9066," History.com, https://www.history.com/this-day-in-history/roosevelt-signs-executive-order-9066 (accessed October 3, 2019).

4 "Table 2: Poverty Status of People by Family Relationship, Race, and Hispanic Origin: 1959 to 2018," U.S. Census Bureau, https://www2.census.gov/programs-surveys/cps/tables/time-series/historical-poverty-people/hstpov2.xls (accessed October 3, 2019).

5 Ibid.

6 Rachel Sheffield and Robert Rector, "The War on Poverty After 50 Years," Heritage Foundation, September 15, 2014, http://www.heritage.org/poverty-and-inequality/report/the-war-poverty-after-50-years (accessed October 3, 2019).

7 Charles M. Blow, "Drug Bust," *New York Times*, June 10, 2011, https://www.nytimes.com/2011/06/11/opinion/11blow.html (accessed October 3, 2019).

8 Serena Dai, "A Chart That Says the War on Drugs Isn't Working," *The Atlantic*, October 12, 2012, https://www.theatlantic.com/national/archive/2012/10/chart-says-war-drugs-isnt-working/322592/ (accessed October 3, 2019).

9 Radley Balko, "Why the 'Wet Tea Leaves' Drug Raid Was Outrageous," *Washington Post*, January 11, 2016, https://www.washingtonpost.com/news/the-watch/wp/2016/01/11/why-the-wet-tea-leaves-drug-raid-was-outrageous/.

10 Kevin Sack, "Door-Busting Drug Raids Leave a Trail of Blood," *New York Times*, March 18, 2017, https://www.nytimes.com/interactive/2017/03/18/us/forced-entry-warrant-drug-raid.html (accessed October 3, 2019).

11 John L. Worrall, "Asset Forfeiture," Center for Problem-Oriented Policing, November 2008, http://www.popcenter.org/Responses/pdfs/asset_forfeiture.pdf (accessed October 3, 2019).

12 Christopher Ingraham, "Law Enforcement Took More Stuff from People Than Burglars Did Last Year," *Washington Post*, November 23, 2015, https://www.washingtonpost.com/news/wonk/wp/2015/11/23/cops-took-more-stuff-from-people-than-burglars-did-last-year/ (accessed October 3, 2019).

13 "DHS Budget," Department of Homeland Security, https://www.dhs.gov/dhs-budget (accessed October 3, 2019).

14 "Mission," Transportation Security Administration, https://www.tsa.gov/about/tsa-mission (accessed October 3, 2019).

15 David Horsey, "TSA's 95% Failure Rate Shows Airport Security Is a Charade," *Los Angeles Times*, June 9, 2015, http://www.latimes.com/opinion/topoftheticket/la-na-tt-tsa-airport-security-charade-20150608-story.html (accessed October 3, 2019).

16 President Barack Obama, Remarks at the National Defense University, May 23, 2013, https://obamawhitehouse.archives.gov/the-press-office/2013/05/23/remarks-president-national-defense-university (accessed October 3, 2019).

17 Starr's 1970 version of the song "War" is the most famous.

## Chapter 7: Taxes

1 All quotes found in "The Byzantine U.S. Tax Code," *CFO Edge*, November 9, 2011, https://www.cfoedge.com/blog/corporate-governance/tax-regulatory-strategy/the-byzantine-u-s-tax-code/ (accessed October 7, 2019).

2 "Annual Report to Congress, 2016: Executive Summary," National Taxpayer Advocate, https://taxpayeradvocate.irs.gov/Media/Default/Documents/2016-ARC/ARC16_ExecSummary.pdf (accessed October 7, 2019).

3 Ibid.

4 "The Tax Burden on Tobacco, 1970–2018," Centers for Disease Control and Prevention, https://chronicdata.cdc.gov/Policy/The-Tax-Burden-on-Tobacco-1970-2018/7nwe-3aj9/data (accessed October 8, 2019).

5 Ibid.

6 Herbert L. Lyon and Julian L. Simon, "Price Elasticity of the Demand for Cigarettes in the United States," *American Journal of Agricultural Economics* 50, no. 4 (November 1968): 888–95, https://academic.oup.com/ajae/article-abstract/50/4/888/116467?redirectedFrom=PDF (accessed October 7, 2019); Craig A. Gallet and John A. List, "Cigarette Demand: A Meta-Analysis of Elasticities," *Health Economics* 12, no. 10 (November 2002): 821–35, https://onlinelibrary.wiley.com/doi/pdf/10.1002/hec.765 (accessed October 21, 2019); "Economic Trends in Tobacco," Centers for Disease Control and Prevention, https://www.cdc.gov/tobacco/data_statistics/fact_sheets/economics/econ_facts/index.htm (accessed October 21, 2019).

7 Walter E. Williams, "Ignorance, Stupidity, or Connivance?" Creators Syndicate, August 10, 2011, http://lewrockwell.com/williams-w/w-williams92.1.html (accessed October 7, 2019).

8   George F. Will, "Tax Break for the Yachting Class," *Washington Post*, October 28, 1999. http://www.washingtonpost.com/wp-srv/WPcap/1999-10/28/010r-102899-idx.html (accessed October 7, 2019).

9   Ibid.

10   Edmund Contoski, "Economically Illiterate Obama, Re: Corporate Jets," Heartland Institute, July 12, 2011, http://blog.heartland.org/2011/07/economically-illiterate-obama-re-corporate-jets/ (accessed October 7, 2019); Will, "Tax Break for the Yachting Class"; Williams, "Ignorance, Stupidity, or Connivance?"

11   "Federal Receipts as Percent of Gross Domestic Product," Federal Reserve Bank of St. Louis, October 25, 2019, https://fred.stlouisfed.org/series/FYFRGDA188S (accessed October 31, 2019).

12   "U.S. Individual Income Tax: Tax Rates for Regular Tax: Highest Bracket," Federal Reserve Bank of St. Louis, December 2, 2016, https://fred.stlouisfed.org/series/IITTRHB (accessed October 7, 2019).

13   "Historical Corporate Top Tax Rate and Bracket: 1909–2018," Tax Policy Center, https://www.taxpolicycenter.org/statistics/corporate-top-tax-rate-and-bracket (accessed October 7, 2019).

14   Kimberly Amadeo, "Capital Gains Tax, Rates, and Impact," *The Balance*, July 22, 2019, https://www.thebalance.com/what-is-the-capital-gains-tax-3305824 (accessed October 7, 2019).

15   "A Historical Look at Estate and Gift Tax Rates: Maximum Estate Tax Rates (1916–2011)," CCH, https://www.cch.com/press/news/historicalestategifttaxrates.pdf (accessed October 7, 2019).

16   "Historical Social Security Tax Rates," Tax Policy Center, July 2019, http://www.taxpolicycenter.org/statistics/payroll-tax-rates (accessed October 7, 2019).

17   Sarah Berger, "Warren Buffett Has Been Making the Same Salary for Decades—and It's Surprisingly Low," CNBC, March 19, 2018, https://www.cnbc.com/2018/03/19/warren-buffetts-berkshire-hathaway-salary.html (accessed October 7, 2019).

18   Eric Felten, "How the Taxman Cleared the Dance Floor," *Wall Street Journal*, March 17, 2013, https://www.wsj.com/articles/SB10001424127887323628804578348050712410108 (accessed October 7, 2019).

19   "The Distribution of Household Income and Federal Taxes, 2013," Congressional Budget Office, June 2016, https://www.cbo.gov/sites/default/files/114th-congress-2015-2016/reports/51361-householdincomefedtaxesonecol.pdf (accessed October 7, 2019).

20   The natural counterargument is that Social Security retirement benefits are in exchange for Social Security taxes. The Supreme Court has ruled clearly on the matter that, despite the political rhetoric, Social Security taxes are not earmarked but are simply part of the general revenue (*Helvering v. Davis*, 1937), and that retirees have no earned right to the benefits (*Flemming v. Nestor*, 1960).

21   "The Distribution of Household Income and Federal Taxes, 2013."

22   Due to rounding, not all figures match exactly the figures that appear in the CBO report. Where there are discrepancies, the magnitude of the discrepancy is less than 1 percent of the figure shown in the table. For those who care to read the CBO report, the CBO uses the following definitions: "Before-Tax Income" is market income plus transfers; "After-Tax Income" is market income plus transfers minus taxes.

23   "Taxes," Gallup, https://news.gallup.com/poll/1714/taxes.aspx (accessed October 7, 2019).

24 Joel Slemrod, "The Role of Misconceptions in Support for Regressive Tax Reform," *National Tax Journal* 59, no. 1 (March 2006): 57–75, https://www.jstor.org/stable/41790312?seq=1#page_scan_tab_contents (accessed October 7, 2019).

25 "The Distribution of Household Income and Federal Taxes, 2013."

26 "Table 1.1—Summary of Receipts, Outlays, and Surpluses or Deficits: 1789–2024," Office of Management and Budget, https://www.whitehouse.gov/omb/historical-tables/ (accessed October 8, 2019). Official debt figures show budget surpluses for the years 1998–2001. But President Clinton, while coming close, did not actually balance the budget. The official figures employ government accounting definitions that classify revenues and expenses in nonstandard ways. Government definitions aside, the federal debt rose in every year of Clinton's administration. The change in the debt is the gold-standard measure of the deficit. The fact that the debt increased indicates that the government was spending more than it collected.

27 "Table 1.1—Summary of Receipts, Outlays, and Surpluses or Deficits: 1789–2024."

28 Even when the top federal tax rate stood at more than 90 percent, people who earned enough to reach that top marginal bracket paid an average tax rate closer to 50 percent.

## Chapter 8: Debt

1 Kimberly Amadeo, "Who Owns the U.S. National Debt?" *The Balance*, July 30, 2019, https://www.thebalance.com/who-owns-the-u-s-national-debt-3306124.

2 Drop to Gallon Conversion, https://www.conversion-metric.org/volume/drop-to-gallon (accessed October 8, 2019). This calculation assumes 58,000 drops of water in a gallon and 660,000 gallons of water in an Olympic-sized pool.

3 This calculation assumes forty blades of grass per square inch.

4 "The Basics of Treasury Securities," TreasuryDirect, https://www.treasurydirect.gov/instit/research/faqs/faqs_basics.htm#why (accessed October 8, 2019).

5 John Mauldin, "Your Pension Is a Lie: There's $210 Trillion of Liabilities Our Government Can't Fulfill," *Forbes*, October 10, 2017, https://www.forbes.com/sites/johnmauldin/2017/10/10/your-pension-is-a-lie-theres-210-trillion-of-liabilities-our-government-cant-fulfill/#1f20973f65b1 (accessed October 8, 2019).

6 "GDP (Current US$)," World Bank, https://data.worldbank.org/indicator/NY.GDP.MKTP.CD (accessed October 8, 2019).

7 Jackie Calmes, "Some of Obama's Favorite Programs to Face Cuts, Budget Director Says," *New York Times*, February 5, 2011, https://www.nytimes.com/2011/02/06/us/politics/06budget.html (accessed October 9, 2019).

8 "Table 1.1—Summary of Receipts, Outlays, and Surpluses or Deficits: 1789–2024," Office of Management and Budget, https://www.whitehouse.gov/omb/historical-tables/ (accessed October 8, 2019).

9 "Average Interest Rates on U.S. Treasury Securities," TreasuryDirect, https://www.treasurydirect.gov/govt/rates/pd/avg/avg.htm (accessed October 8, 2019).

10 Some economists claim that the government does not calculate its interest costs correctly. But economists' estimates of the government's interest costs in the recent past are not markedly dissimilar from the government's reported interest costs. Regardless, the point remains that (on average) higher interest rates cost the government more in interest expense, no matter how one calculates the interest expense. See Thomas Sargent and George Hall, "Net Interest Payments on the Federal Debt:

A Flawed Measure," VoxEU.org, February 17, 2010, http://www.voxeu.org/article/ net-interest-payments-federal-debt-flawed-measure (accessed October 8, 2019).

11   Amy Belasco, "The Cost of Iraq, Afghanistan, and Other Global War on Ter-ror Operations Since 9/11," *Congressional Research Service*, December 8, 2014, https://www.fas.org/sgp/crs/natsec/RL33110.pdf (accessed October 8, 2019).

12   "Table 1.1—Summary of Receipts, Outlays, and Surpluses or Deficits: 1789–2024."

13   "The 2019 Annual Report of the Board of Trustees of the Federal Old-Age and Survivors Insurance and Federal Disability Insurance Trust Funds," https://www. ssa.gov/OACT/TR/2019/tr2019.pdf (accessed October 8, 2019).

14   D. Andrew Austin, "The Debt Limit: History and Recent Increases," *Congressio-nal Research Service*, February 13, 2013, https://fas.org/sgp/crs/misc/RL31967.pdf (accessed October 8, 2019).

15   Jeanne Sahadi, "Debt Ceiling FAQs: What You Need to Know," CNN/*Money*, May 18, 2011, https://money.cnn.com/2011/01/03/news/economy/debt_ceiling_ faqs/index.htm (accessed October 8, 2019).

16   Scott Greenberg, "Summary of the Latest Federal Income Tax Data, 2015 Update," Tax Foundation, November 19, 2015, https://taxfoundation.org/summary-latest-federal-income-tax-data-2015-update/.

17   "Table 1.1—Summary of Receipts, Outlays, and Surpluses or Deficits: 1789–2024."

18   "The Distribution of Household Income and Federal Taxes, 2013," Congressional Budget Office, June 2016, https://www.cbo.gov/sites/default/files/114th-congress-2015-2016/ reports/51361-householdincomefedtaxesonecol.pdf (accessed October 8, 2019).

19   CPI Inflation Calculator, Bureau of Labor Statistics, https://data.bls.gov/cgi-bin/ cpicalc.pl?cost1=1.00&year1=197501&year2=201907 (accessed October 8, 2019).

20   "M1 Money Stock," Federal Reserve Bank of St. Louis, October 3, 2019, https:// fred.stlouisfed.org/series/M1 (accessed October 8, 2019).

21   "Real Gross Domestic Product," Federal Reserve Bank of St. Louis, September 26, 2019, https://fred.stlouisfed.org/series/GDPC1 (accessed October 8, 2019).

22   "Population," Federal Reserve Bank of St. Louis, September 27, 2019, https://fred. stlouisfed.org/series/POPTHM (accessed October 8, 2019).

23   Thomas E. Woods Jr., "The Great Gold Robbery of 1933," *Mises Daily*, August 13, 2008, https://mises.org/library/great-gold-robbery-1933 (accessed October 8, 2019).

24   "Gross Domestic Product," Federal Reserve Bank of St. Louis, October 30, 2019, https://fred.stlouisfed.org/series/GDP (accessed October 31, 2019).

25   "Federal Receipts as Percent of Gross Domestic Product," Federal Reserve Bank of St. Louis, October 25, 2019, https://fred.stlouisfed.org/series/FYFRGDA188S (accessed October 31, 2019).

26   As noted in chapter 7, although official debt figures show budget surpluses for the years 1998–2001, the federal debt increased in those years, meaning that the gov-ernment spent more than it collected. The supposed surplus reflected the nonstan-dard ways government accounting classifies revenue and expenses.

## Chapter 9: Busybullies

1   "Message from Sylvia Burwell, Secretary, U.S. Department of Health and Human Services," *E-Cigarette Use Among Youth and Young Adults: A Report of the Surgeon*

*General* (U.S. Department of Health and Human Services, 2016), https://www.cdc.gov/tobacco/basic_information/e-cigarettes/Quick-Facts-on-the-Risks-of-E-cigarettes-for-Kids-Teens-and-Young-Adults.html#one (accessed October 21, 2019).

2    "Deaths: Final Data for 2017," *National Vital Statistics Reports* 68, no. 9 (June 24, 2019), https://www.cdc.gov/nchs/data/nvsr/nvsr68/nvsr68_09-508.pdf (accessed October 21, 2019)

3    Lindsey Tanner, "Increasing Number of Vaping U.S. Teens Is Found to Be Fueled by Juul and Mint," Associated Press, November 7, 2019, https://www.post-gazette.com/news/health/2019/11/06/vaping-flavors-mint-Juul-teens/stories/201911050168 (accessed November 10, 2019).

4    Karen A. Cullen et al., "E-Cigarette Use Among Youth in the United States," *Journal of the American Medical Association (JAMA)*, Supplementary Online Content, November 5, 2019, https://jamanetwork.com/journals/jama/article-abstract/2755265 (accessed November 6, 2019).

5    "Legal Recreational Marijuana States and DC," ProCon.org, https://marijuana.procon.org/view.resource.php?resourceID=006868 (accessed October 9, 2019); "Legal Medical Marijuana States and DC," ProCon.org, https://medicalmarijuana.procon.org/view.resource.php?resourceID=000881 (accessed October 9, 2019).

6    "The Sad Anniversary of Big Commercial Pot," *Colorado Springs Gazette*, November 9, 2017, https://gazette.com/editorial-the-sad-anniversary-of-big-commercial-pot/article_fd933a7d-c572-5e80-99cb-81216e3465e2.html (accessed October 9, 2019).

7    Rae Ellen Bichell, "Scientists Still Seek a Reliable DUI Test for Marijuana," NPR, July 30, 2017, https://www.npr.org/sections/health-shots/2017/07/30/523004450/scientists-still-seek-a-reliable-dui-test-for-marijuana (accessed October 9, 2019).

8    "National Survey on Drug Use and Health: Comparison of 2014–2015 and 2015–2016 Population Percentages (50 States and the District of Columbia)," Substance Abuse and Mental Health Services Administration, https://www.samhsa.gov/data/sites/default/files/NSDUHsaeShortTermCHG2016/NSDUHsaeShortTermCHG2016.pdf (accessed October 9, 2019).

9    "Key Substance Use and Mental Health Indicators in the United States: Results from the 2016 National Survey on Drug Use and Health," Substance Abuse and Mental Health Services Administration, September 2017, https://www.samhsa.gov/data/sites/default/files/NSDUH-FFR1-2016/NSDUH-FFR1-2016.pdf (accessed October 9, 2019).

10   Jacqueline Howard, "Recreational Marijuana Legalization Tied to Decline in Teens Using Pot, Study Says," CNN, July 8, 2019, https://www.cnn.com/2019/07/08/health/recreational-marijuana-laws-teens-study/index.html (accessed October 10, 2019).

11   Lisa Rough, "How to Open a Medical Marijuana Dispensary or Recreational Cannabis Shop in Colorado," *Leafly*, June 18, 2015, https://www.leafly.com/news/industry/how-to-open-a-medical-marijuana-dispensary-or-recreational-cannab (accessed October 9, 2019).

12   "Justice Department Issues Memo on Marijuana Enforcement," Department of Justice, January 4, 2018, https://www.justice.gov/opa/pr/justice-department-issues-memo-marijuana-enforcement (accessed November 6, 2019).

13   C.J. Ciaramella, "Jeff Sessions Says Opioid Addiction Starts with Marijuana. Here Are 6 Studies That Say Otherwise," *Reason*, February 7, 2018, https://reason.com/2018/02/07/jeff-sessions-says-opioid-addiction-star/ (accessed November 6, 2019).

14  "Is Marijuana a Gateway Drug?" National Institute on Drug Abuse, September 2019, https://www.drugabuse.gov/publications/research-reports/marijuana/marijuana-gateway-drug (accessed October 10, 2019). The National Institute on Drug Abuse reports: "Some research suggests that marijuana use is likely to precede use of other licit and illicit substances and the development of addiction to other substances.... However, the majority of people who use marijuana do not go on to use other, 'harder' substances. Also, cross-sensitization is not unique to marijuana. Alcohol and nicotine also prime the brain for a heightened response to other drugs and are, like marijuana, also typically used before a person progresses to other, more harmful substances.... An alternative to the gateway-drug hypothesis is that people who are more vulnerable to drug-taking are simply more likely to start with readily available substances such as marijuana, tobacco, or alcohol, and their subsequent social interactions with others who use drugs increases their chances of trying other drugs." See also Roberto Secades-Villa et al., "Probability and Predictors of the Cannabis Gateway Effect: A National Study," *International Journal on Drug Policy* 26, no. 2 (February 2015): 135–42, https://www.ncbi.nlm.nih.gov/pubmed/25168081 (accessed October 10, 2019).

15  Christopher Ingraham, "Trump's Pick for Attorney General: 'Good People Don't Smoke Marijuana,'" *Washington Post*, November 18, 2016, https://www.washingtonpost.com/news/wonk/wp/2016/11/18/trumps-pick-for-attorney-general-good-people-dont-smoke-marijuana/?utm_term=.f3694577fd88 (accessed October 9, 2019).

16  C.J. Ciaramella, "Here's That Time Jeff Sessions Wanted to Execute Drug Dealers," *Reason*, February 1, 2017, http://reason.com/blog/2017/02/01/heres-that-time-jeff-sessions-wanted-to (accessed October 9, 2019).

17  Christopher Ingraham, "Jeff Sessions Personally Asked Congress to Let Him Prosecute Medical-Marijuana Providers," *Washington Post*, June 13, 2017, https://www.washingtonpost.com/news/wonk/wp/2017/06/13/jeff-sessions-personally-asked-congress-to-let-him-prosecute-medical-marijuana-providers/ (accessed October 10, 2019).

18  Adam K. Raymond, "Jeff Sessions Says Marijuana Is 'Only Slightly Less Awful' Than Heroin," *New York*, March 15, 2017, http://nymag.com/daily/intelligencer/2017/03/sessions-marijuana-is-slightly-less-awful-than-heroin.html (accessed October 9, 2019).

19  Evan Halper, "Trump Administration Abandons Crackdown on Legal Marijuana," *Los Angeles Times*, April 13, 2018, https://www.latimes.com/politics/la-na-pol-marijuana-trump-20180413-story.html (accessed October 10, 2019).

20  Alex Berenson, "What Advocates of Legalizing Pot Don't Want You to Know," *New York Times*, January 4, 2019, https://www.nytimes.com/2019/01/04/opinion/marijuana-pot-health-risks-legalization.html (accessed October 10, 2019).

21  Ruibin Lu et al., "The Cannabis Effect on Crime: Time-Series Analysis of Crime in Colorado and Washington State," *Justice Quarterly*, October 8, 2019, https://www.tandfonline.com/doi/full/10.1080/07418825.2019.1666903 (accessed October 10, 2019); Jacob Sullum, "Study Finds Marijuana Legalization Had Little Impact on Crime in Colorado or Washington," *Reason*, October 8, 2019, https://reason.com/2019/10/08/study-finds-marijuana-legalization-had-little-impact-on-crime-in-colorado-or-washington/ (accessed October 10, 2019).

22  See Antony Davies and James R. Harrigan, "Marijuana Doomsday Didn't Come," *U.S. News and World Report*, December 19, 2017, https://www.usnews.com/opinion/economic-intelligence/articles/2017-12-19/marijuana-legalization-doomsday-didnt-come-to-colorado (accessed October 21, 2019).

23   "Table 1: Crime in the United States by Volume and Rate per 100,000 Inhabitants, 1997–2016," Uniform Crime Report, FBI, https://ucr.fbi.gov/crime-in-the-u.s/2016/crime-in-the-u.s.-2016/tables/table-1 (accessed October 9, 2019).

24   Point in Time Reports, Metro Denver Homeless Initiative, https://www.mdhi.org/pit_reports (accessed November 19, 2019).

25   "Drug War Statistics," Drug Policy Alliance, http://www.drugpolicy.org/issues/drug-war-statistics (accessed October 9, 2019).

26   Christopher Ingraham, "Police Arrest More People for Marijuana Use Than for All Violent Crimes—Combined," *Washington Post*, October 12, 2016, https://www.washingtonpost.com/news/wonk/wp/2016/10/12/police-arrest-more-people-for-marijuana-use-than-for-all-violent-crimes-combined/ (accessed October 9, 2019).

27   Mattie Quinn, "Is Porn a Public Health Crisis? 16 States Say Yes," *Governing*, July 19, 2019, https://www.governing.com/topics/health-human-services/gov-pornography-public-health-crisis-states.html (accessed October 11, 2019); Lucy Westcott, "Utah Becomes First State to Declare Pornography a Public Health Hazard," *Newsweek*, April 20, 2016, https://www.newsweek.com/utah-porn-public-health-hazard-450223 (accessed October 11, 2019); "South Dakota Lawmakers Decry Pornography as Health Risk," Associated Press, January 24, 2017, https://www.ksfy.com/content/news/South-Dakota-lawmakers-decry-pornography-as-health-risk-411685145.html (accessed October 11, 2019).

28   Jared Brey and Holly Otterbein, "The No-Bullshit Guide to the Fight Over the Philly Soda Tax," *Philadelphia Magazine*, June 8, 2016, https://www.phillymag.com/citified/2016/06/08/soda-tax-no-bullshit-guide/ (accessed October 9, 2019).

29   John Rawlins, "Stores See Initial Impact of Philadelphia's Soda Tax," 6ABC.com, January 31, 2017, https://6abc.com/news/stores-see-initial-impact-of-philadelphias-soda-tax/1730598/ (accessed October 9, 2019).

30   Eric Boehm, "Outrage in Philadelphia as New Soda Tax Doubles Drink Prices," *Reason*, January 5, 2017, https://reason.com/blog/2017/01/05/soda-tax-sparks-outrage-in-philadelphia (accessed October 9, 2019); Julia Terruso, "Soda Companies, Supermarkets Report 30–50 Pct. Sales Drop from Soda Tax," *Philadelphia Inquirer*, February 21, 2017, https://www.inquirer.com/philly/news/Soda-companies-supermarkets-report-50-percent-losses-from-soda-tax.html (accessed October 9, 2019).

31   Morgan Zalot, "Former Philadelphia Police Commissioner Ramsey: 'We Are Sitting on a Powder Keg,'" NBC Philadelphia, July 10, 2016, https://www.nbcphiladelphia.com/news/local/Charles-Ramsey-Powder-keg-Police-Protests-Meet-Press-Chuck-Todd-386206691.html (accessed October 9, 2019).

32   Ray Sanchez, "Choke Hold by Cop Killed NY Man, Medical Examiner Says," CNN, August 2, 2014, https://www.cnn.com/2014/08/01/justice/new-york-choke-hold-death/index.html (accessed October 9, 2019).

## Chapter 10: Cooperation

1   President Thomas Jefferson, First Inaugural Address, March 4, 1801, http://www.presidency.ucsb.edu/ws/index.php?pid=25803 (accessed October 16, 2019).

2   The Fraser Institute measures economic freedom by asking how free people are to use and exchange their property with others and to hold that property free of the threat of force, fraud, or theft. According to Fraser, a society is more economically

free when that society protects people's property rights, treats people as being equal in the eyes of the law, enforces contracts in an evenhanded manner, maintains a stable monetary system (i.e., prevents the monetary authority from stealing people's property through inflation), imposes a lighter tax burden on people, erects fewer barriers to trade, and relies more on cooperation rather than coercion to allocate resources and production. Fraser quantifies these by combining forty-two measures from third-party sources such as the International Country Risk Guide, the World Economic Forum, the World Bank, and state and national governments into an index that represents the degree of economic freedom in a society at a point in time. For comparisons among the U.S. states, we use Fraser's subnational index measuring overall freedom. Fraser recommends using the subnational metric for cross-state comparisons.

3    "Historical Income Tables: Households, Table H-8," U.S. Census Bureau, https://www.census.gov/data/tables/time-series/demo/income-poverty/historical-income-households.html (accessed July 8, 2018); Dean Stansel, José Torra, and Fred McMahon, *Economic Freedom of North America 2017* (Fraser Institute, 2017), https://www.fraserinstitute.org/studies/economic-freedom-of-north-america-2017 (accessed July 8, 2018).

4    "Historical Poverty Tables: People and Families—1959 to 2018," U.S. Census Bureau, https://www.census.gov/data/tables/time-series/demo/income-poverty/historical-poverty-people.html (accessed October 18, 2019); "Interactive Data: GDP and Personal Income, Regional Data," U.S. Bureau of Economic Analysis, https://apps.bea.gov/itable/iTable.cfm?ReqID=70&step=1 (accessed July 8, 2018); Stansel, Torra, and McMahon, *Economic Freedom of North America 2017*.

5    U.S. Census Bureau, Current Population Survey, Table Generator, https://www.census.gov/cps/data/cpstablecreator.html; Stansel, Torra, and McMahon, *Economic Freedom of North America 2017*.

6    North Korea does not release economic figures. Estimates of the size of its economy vary. See Alex McIntyre and Adrian Leung, "How Big Is North Korea's Economy? Pick a Number, Any Number," *Bloomberg*, https://www.bloomberg.com/graphics/2018-north-korea-economy-size/ (accessed October 18, 2019).

7    Richard Knight, "Are North Koreans Really Three Inches Shorter Than South Koreans?," BBC News, April 23, 2012, https://www.bbc.com/news/magazine-17774210 (accessed October 18, 2019).

8    World Factbook, CIA, https://www.cia.gov/library/publications/the-world-factbook/geos/ks.html (accessed October 18, 2019).

9    Rick Newman, "Here's How Lousy Life Is in North Korea," *U.S. News and World Report*, April 12, 2013, https://www.usnews.com/news/blogs/rick-newman/2013/04/12/heres-how-lousy-life-is-in-north-korea (accessed October 18, 2019).

10   "Poverty Headcount Ratio at $1.90 a Day (2011 PPP) (% of Population)," World Bank, https://data.worldbank.org/indicator/SI.POV.DDAY (accessed July 9, 2018); "Economic Freedom Rankings," Fraser Institute, https://www.fraserinstitute.org/economic-freedom/dataset (accessed July 9, 2018). World Bank defines the "extreme poverty rate" as the fraction of a country's population that lives on less than $1.90 per day (adjusted for inflation and differences in costs of living). Because not all countries report data, the available data range across the years from a low of ten countries to a high of seventy-nine countries. From 2003 forward, more than fifty countries reported for each year.

11  Not all countries report poverty rates. Prior to 2002, fewer than ten countries in each year satisfied the criteria of having below median per capita GDP and reporting poverty rates. From 2002 forward, fifteen or more countries reported. The poverty rates were higher for these countries than for all other countries combined.

12  "Poverty Headcount Ratio at $1.90 a Day (2011 PPP) (% of Population)"; "Economic Freedom Rankings."

13  Todd Moss and Gailyn Portelance, "The World Bank Now Has Three Poverty Lines. Why Not Three for Energy?" Center for Global Development, November 9, 2017, https://www.cgdev.org/blog/world-bank-now-has-three-poverty-lines-why-not-three-energy (accessed October 21, 2019).

14  "GDP Per Capita (Constant 2010 US$)," World Bank, https://data.worldbank.org/indicator/NY.GDP.PCAP.KD (accessed October 21, 2019); "Economic Freedom Rankings." Prior to 1980, the number of poor countries that reported data were very low, ranging from twenty to twenty-one. From 1980 to 2015, the number of poor countries reporting rose from thirty to more than fifty.

15  See https://development-data-hub-s3-public.s3.amazonaws.com/ddhfiles/94536/all-ginis_2013.xls; "Economic Freedom Rankings." From 1983 through 2010, the number of reporting countries varied by year from a low of twenty-one to a high of eighty-one.

16  "Human Development Data (1990–2017): Gender Inequality Index," United Nations Development Programme, http://hdr.undp.org/en/data (accessed October 21, 2019); "Economic Freedom Rankings."

17  "Human Development Data (1990–2017): Gender Inequality Index"; "Economic Freedom Rankings."

18  "Child Labour," UN Data, http://data.un.org/Data.aspx?d=SOWC&f=inID%3A86 (accessed October 21, 2019); "Economic Freedom Rankings." The UN reports one number for each country over the period 2002 through 2011. In the chart, we separate those numbers into two groups for each year based on which countries fell into the more cooperative or more coercive categories that year. Therefore, the changes in the bars over time show not changes in child labor rates but changes in the memberships of the two country groups.

19  William J. O'Neil Center for Global Markets and Freedom, SMU Cox School of Business, 2014–15 Annual Report, *The Wealth of Cities: Pursuing Economic Freedom Closer to Home*, https://www.smu.edu/~/media/Site/Cox/CentersAndInstitutes/ONeilCenter/Research/AnnualReports/2014-15_annual_report_full.ashx (accessed October 21, 2019).

20  "Table 1.1—Summary of Receipts, Outlays, and Surpluses or Deficits: 1789–2024," Office of Management and Budget, https://www.whitehouse.gov/omb/historical-tables/ (accessed October 21, 2019).

# ACKNOWLEDGMENTS

We wish to thank the following for comments on earlier drafts of this work: Professor Robert M. S. McDonald, Professor James Stacey Taylor, Professor Howard Baetjer, Peter Wentz, and Andra Mount. We also thank Peter Wentz for his unparalleled hospitality in giving us beds and food for a week as we hammered out our final draft. We also thank the many members of the *Words & Numbers* Backstage Facebook group (self-named, "the W&Nkers"), who keep our corner of the internet populated with sane, polite, and interesting ideas.

# INDEX

Adams, Jerome, 155
Adult Basic Education Grants, 107
Affordable Care Act (ACA or Obama-
    care), 36, 41, 44, 122
Afghanistan, 110, 140
Aid for Graduate and Professional Study
    for Disadvantaged and Minorities, 107
Alaska, 94, 97
Americans with Disabilities Act, 29–30
Amtrak, 59
Aristophanes, 20
Aristotle, 11, 14–15
Arizona, 28, 56
Arkansas, 167
Assets for Independence, 106
Athens, Greece, 20
Atlanta, GA, 66, 99
Australia, 26, 99–100
Australian Institute of Criminology,
    99–100

Bachus, Spencer, 120
Berkshire Hathaway, 126

Biden, Joe, 85
"Bill for the More General Diffusion of
    Knowledge, A," 42
Bill of Rights, 38, 40, 43
Black Codes, 83–84
Boston, MA, 114
Brady, James, 84–85
Brady, Sarah, 84
Brady Bill, 84
Brazil, 99
Buffett, Warren, 126
bureaucrats, 24, 26, 31, 48–49, 55–59
Bureau of Alcohol, Tobacco, and Fire-
    arms, 84
Bureau of Economic Analysis, 168
Bureau of Justice Statistics, 93–100
Bureau of Labor Statistics, 72–75, 78
Bush, George H. W., 123
Bush, George W., 113
businesses, 9–11, 29–31, 47–48, 58,
    64–67, 70, 74, 78, 121, 123, 126,
    129, 144, 157

CCH Inc., 120
Centers for Disease Control and Prevention (CDC), 90, 95–98, 100
Chaerephon, 20
Chicago, IL, 99
Childcare and Child Development Block Grant, 108
Childcare Entitlement to the States, 108
Child Care Food Program, 107
Choi, Brian, 66–70
Civil War, 44, 83, 105
Clinton, Bill, 84, 133
*Code of Federal Regulations*, 25, 45–46
Colorado, 156–59
*Colorado Springs Gazette*, the, 156
Commodity Supplemental Food Program, 107
Communications Workers of America, 79
Community Development Block Grant and Related Development Funds, 108
Community Service Block Grant, 107
Congress, 71, 84, 90, 109, 111, 120–21, 123, 138–39, 143, 148–49, 158
Congressional Budget Office (CBO), 127, 129–30
Consolidated Health Center/Community Health Centers, 106
Constitution, U.S. 38, 104, 111–12, 150

Davis, Trevor, 115
Declaration of Independence, 13, 38
democracy, 10, 15, 50–51
Democrats, 21, 81
Department of Appalachian Regional Development, 108
Department of Justice, 112
Department of Labor, 67
Department of Motor Vehicles (DMV), 57
Department of Veterans Affairs (VA), 56–57
dictatorship, 10
Dominican Republic, 170

Earned Income Tax Credit, 106, 129
Economic Development Administration, 108

economy, 44–45, 124–26, 134, 140, 143–44, 146–47, 149, 170, 177
Education for Homeless Children and Youth, 107
Emergency Banking Act of 1933, 149
Emergency Food and Shelter Program, 107
Empowerment Zones, 108
English language, 34
Enterprise Communities Renewal, 108
Even Start, 107

Family Planning, 107
Farmers' Market Nutrition Program, 107
*Federalist*, 38
Federal Reserve, 44–46, 139–40, 146–48
Federal Reserve Bank of St. Louis, 44–46
FedEx, 59
Finland, 99
Food Stamp Employment and Training Program, 107
Foster Grandparents, 107
Fraser Institute, 165–75

Gallup, 92–94, 131
Garner, Eric, 161
Gear-Up, 107
General Assistance, 106
General Assistance to Indians, 106
George, Andy, 23–24
Georgia, 92, 111
Gini Index, 172–73
government: and busybullies, 151–54, 156, 159–62; as a coercive organization, 10–14; and cooperation, 164–66, 169, 174, 176–78; and debt, 135–50; and gun control, 84, 90; and its proper role, 14–16, 37–46; and minimum wage, 66–68, 71–72, 76, 79, 81; and taxes, 120–28, 130–34; and wars on poverty, drugs, and terror, 103–4, 106, 108–11, 113, 116; and unintended consequences, 19–29, 31, 47–48, 50, 53–59; in Venezuela, 31–32
Gratia, Al, 87

Great Britain, 38
Great Depression, 150
Great Recession, 150
Green Bay Packers, 115
Gun Control Act of 1968, 84

Haiti, 170
Hamilton, Alexander, 38
Hanoi, 27
happiness, 11–13, 24, 39, 49, 53, 55, 57, 67
Hawaii, 94
Hayek, Friedrich, 33
Head Start, 108
Healthy Marriage and Responsible
    Fatherhood Grants, 107
Healthy Start, 106
Hennard, George, 87–88, 92
Herman, Melinda, 92
Herzberg, Elaine, 29
Hinckley, John, Jr., 84
Hispaniola, 170
Home Investment Partnership Program,
    107
Homeland Security, 113–14, 16
Homeless Assistance Grants, 107
House of Representatives, U.S., 139
Housing for the Elderly, 107
Hoy No Circula, 30
human beings, humanity, 9–12, 14–16,
    19–20, 24–25, 28, 32–36, 38–39,
    46, 48–49, 53, 55, 57, 59, 68–69,
    87–88, 91, 104–5, 107, 126, 151–53,
    163–64, 178
Hupp, Suzanna, 87–88, 92

Idaho, 97, 167
Independent Living (Chafee Foster Care
    Independence Program), 107–8
Independent Living Training Vouchers,
    108
Independents, 21
India, 27
Iraq, 140
IRS, 119–20

JAMA Pediatrics, 157
Jefferson, Thomas, 13–14, 37–39, 42,
    165, 176

Job Corps, 107
Johnson, Lyndon, 105–6, 110
Joint Committee on Taxation, 123
Jones, Walter, 120

Kansas, 110, 167
Kant, Immanuel, 11
Kennedy, John F., 84
Kentucky, 167
Killeen, TX, 87
knowledge problem, 20, 25, 32–33, 35,
    134, 151, 154
Korean War, 103, 105

LEAP (formerly State Student Incentive
    Grant Program), 107
Legal Services Block Grant, 107
Lincoln, Abraham, 105
Logan International Airport, 114
Los Angeles Times, the, 158
Low-Income Home Energy Assistance
    Program (LIHEAP), 107
Low-Income Housing Tax Credit for
    Developers, 107
Luby's Cafeteria, 87–88, 92

Make Work Pay Tax Credit, 106
Marijuana Accountability Coalition, 156
Marjory Stoneman Douglas High
    School, 89
Marshall County High School, 89
Maryland, 97, 167
Massachusetts, 94–95, 97
Maternal, Infant, and Early Childhood
    Home Visiting Program, 108
Maternal and Child Health, 106
Mathews, Maurice, 66–70
Mathews, Willie, 66–70
median voter theorem, 54
Medicaid, 41, 44
Medical Assistance to Refugees, 106
Medical General Assistance, 106
Medicare, 41, 44, 106, 125, 134, 138
Mexico City, Mexico, 30
Miami, FL, 114
Migrant Education, 107
Migrant Training, 107
military, 41, 53–54, 104, 110–11, 132

Mill, John Stuart, 11
minimum wage, 63–81, 153: hurts marginal workers, 64–66, 77, 81; hurts small business owners, 64, 66–67, 70
Mississippi, 97
Montana, 94, 97
*Mother Jones*, 90, 94

National Academies' Institute of Medicine, 90
National Defense University, 116
National Research Council, 90–91
National Survey on Drug Use and Health, 156
National Taxpayer Advocate, 120
Native American Housing with Disabilities, 107
Native American Training, 107
Nebraska, 97
Needy Families, 107
New Hampshire, 95
New Jersey, 79, 94
New York City, 113, 161
New Zealand, 26
Nicaragua, 34
Nicaraguan Sign Language, 34
Nixon, Richard, 109, 113
Northern Illinois University, 89
North Korea, 169–70
Nutrition Program for the Elderly, 107

Obama, Barack, 64, 85, 90, 116, 122, 139
Obamacare. *See* Affordable Care Act
Office of Management and Budget, 44–46
Olson, Nina, 121
Oracle at Delphi, 20
Oregon, 79
*Oxford English Dictionary, The*, 34

Paine, Thomas, 12–14, 37
Paris, France, 114, 117
Patient Protection and Affordable Care Act. *See* Affordable Care Act
Pell Grants, 107
Philadelphia, PA, 97, 160
Phoenix, AZ, 51–52, 56

Pittsburgh, PA, 97
Plato, 20
politicians, 21, 24, 26, 30–31, 40, 44, 48–49, 53–55, 58–59, 64, 68–69, 71, 73–74, 76, 78, 80–81, 85, 88, 102, 104, 116, 121, 127, 133–35, 138–40, 142, 144–46, 148–50
Portman, Rob, 119
public bureaucrats, 24, 26, 31, 48–49, 55–59
Public Housing, 107
Puerto Rico, 57

Read, Leonard, 21–23
Reagan, Ronald, 84, 108
Refugee Assistance, 106
Refundable Child Credit, 106
Reid, Richard, 114
Republicans, 21, 64
rights, 13–14, 37–47, 89, 104, 112–13, 116, 166; negative rights, 40–43, 46–47; positive rights, 40–47
Riley, Justin Luke, 156
Roosevelt, Franklin, 37, 43–47, 105
Rose Garden, 69
Rural Housing Insurance Fund, 107
Rural Housing Service, 107

Safe and Stable Families, 107
Salem witch trials, 15
Sandy Hook Elementary School, 89
Santa Fe High School, 89
School Breakfast, 107
School Lunch Program, 106–7
Second Amendment, 83–84
Second Bill of Rights (Economic Bill of Rights), 43, 46–47
Secretary of the Treasury, 149
Section 8 Housing, 107
Senate, U.S., 139
Senior Community Service Employment, 107
Sessions, Jeff, 158
Simpson, Homer, 37
Slater, Paul, 92
Slemrod, Joel, 132
Social Security, 41, 44, 55, 106, 125, 129, 134, 136–38, 142, 146

Social Services for Refugees, Asylees, and Humanitarian Cases, 107
society, 10, 12–15, 49–51, 53, 133–34, 159, 161, 163–66, 173, 176
Socrates, 20–21, 24
South Carolina, 167
South Dakota, 160
South Korea, 169–70
Southwest, 59
Sowell, Thomas, 53
Special Milk Program, 107
Special Programs for Disadvantaged Students, 107
Special Supplemental Nutrition Program for Women, Infants, and Children (WIC), 107
Starr, Edwin, 116
State Children's Health Insurance Program (SCHIP), 106
State Housing Expenditures, 107
State of the Union address, 43, 64, 105, 108
Streisand, Barbra, 26
Supplemental Education Opportunity Grants, 107
Supplemental Nutrition Assistance Program (SNAP, formerly Food Stamps), 106
Supreme Court, 105
Switzerland, 99

TANF Block Grant Child Care, 108
TANF Block Grant Services, 107
TANF Work Activities and Training, 107
Temporary Assistance for Needy Families (TANF, formerly Aid to Families with Dependent Children), 106
Temporary Emergency Food Program (TEFAP), 107
Texas, 85, 87–88, 92
Thirteenth Amendment, 83
Thwaites, Thomas, 23–24
Title I Grants to Local Education Authorities, 107
Title III Aging Americans Act, 107
Title IV-E Adoption Assistance, 106
Title IV-E Foster Care, 106

Title XX Social Services Block Grant, 107
Trail of Tears, 15
Transportation Security Administration (TSA), 113–16
Truman, Harry, 105
Trump, Donald, 157–58
Tullock, Gordon, 28
Twenty-First Century Learning Centers, 107

Uber, 28
Umpqua Community College, 89
Unemployment Insurance, 44
United Kingdom, 23
United Nations Development Programme (UNDP), 173–75
United States, 10, 12, 21, 25, 32, 38, 41, 54, 72, 74, 79, 83–84, 90–91, 99–101, 103–6, 108–10, 114–15, 121, 124, 132, 140, 147, 149, 159, 165, 176–77
Universal Service Fund Subsidized Low-Income Phone Service, 107
University of Michigan, 132
USA Today, 56
U.S. Census Bureau, 106, 167–69
U.S. Postal Service, 58–59
Utah, 97, 159

Vasquez, Rafaela, 28–29
Venezuela, 31–32
Vermont, 95
Vietnam War, 103–4
Virginia Tech, 89
voters, voting, 10, 14, 42, 48–55, 58–59, 80, 102, 127, 133–34, 139, 142, 144–45, 150, 152, 177

war on drugs, 109–10
war on poverty, 105–6, 108, 110
war on terror, 113, 116
Washington, 167
Washington, D.C., 120, 139, 147
WIA Adult Employment and Training (formerly JTPA IIA Training for Disadvantaged Adults and Youth), 107

WIA Youth Opportunity Grants (formerly Summer Youth Employment), 107
Wikipedia, 24
World Bank, 170–73
World Trade Center, 113
World War I, 44, 143

World War II, 44, 103–5, 140
Wyoming, 94

Xenophon, 20

Ylioja, Thomas, 155
YouthBuild, 107

# ABOUT THE AUTHORS

**Antony Davies** is the Milton Friedman Distinguished Fellow at the Foundation for Economic Education (FEE) and associate professor of economics at Duquesne University. The cohost of the weekly podcast *Words & Numbers*, he writes frequently for the *Philadelphia Inquirer* and the *Pittsburgh Tribune-Review*, and he also has written for the *Wall Street Journal*, the *Los Angeles Times*, the *Washington Post*, and many other publications. His YouTube videos on economics, government, and policy have garnered millions of views. Dr. Davies lectures on economics at high schools and colleges across the country.

**James R. Harrigan** is managing director of the Freedom Center at the University of Arizona and the F. A. Hayek Distinguished Fellow at the Foundation for Economic Education (FEE). He cohosts the *Words & Numbers* podcast and has written for the *Wall Street Journal*, *USA Today*, the *Philadelphia Inquirer*, and a host of other outlets. Previously, Dr. Harrigan served as dean of the American University of Iraq, Sulaimani; director of academic programs at the Institute for Humane Studies; and senior research fellow at Strata. He lectures on politics and economics at high schools and colleges across the country.

You've read their book.
Now listen to their podcast.

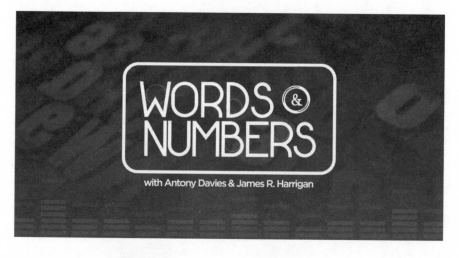

Every week on the *Words & Numbers* podcast,
Antony Davies and James R. Harrigan talk about the
economics and political science of current events.

Check out *Words & Numbers* to discover why
Antony and James have attracted thousands
of devoted listeners to their podcast.

www.wordsandnumbers.org